I0813401

TO

....

FROM

....

DATE

....

Yearlong Inspiration, Encouragement, and Hope

Print ISBN 979-8-89151-168-2

Daily devotions are from *365 Days of Encouragement and Hope for Women*, published by Barbour Publishing, Inc. Prayers are written by Janice Thompson.

Published by Barbour Publishing, Inc., 1810 Barbour Drive, Uhrichsville, Ohio 44683, www.barbourbooks.com

Our mission is to inspire the world with the life-changing message of the Bible.

Printed in China.

HOPE, INSPIRATION, AND ENCOURAGEMENT ALL YEAR LONG

I pray that God, the source of hope, will fill you completely with joy and peace because you trust in him.

ROMANS 15:13 NLT

This lovely daily devotional offers just-right-sized readings that are a perfect fit for your busy lifestyle. These 365 readings feature themes that are important to your heart—including faith, friendship, joy, love, rest, trust, peace, security, and dozens more. As you move through the pages of *One Devotion a Day for Women*, you'll be comforted and inspired every day of the year as you experience the refreshing peace and assurance that can only be found through an intimate relationship with the Master Creator.

Day 1

DANCING IN THE PUDDLES

And so, Lord, where do I put my hope? My only hope is in you.
PSALM 39:7 NLT

They say you can tell a lot about a person's foundation of hope by the way she handles a rainy day. Does she turn into a Gloomy Gertie, wailing, "Oh, woe is me. . ."? Or does she make the best of a bad situation? A hope-filled person will realize that abundant life in Christ isn't just about enduring the storm—it's also about learning to dance in the puddles. So grab your galoshes, and let's boogie!

PRAYER

Lord, I confess that sometimes I whine about the proverbial rainy days I face. I carry on with a sour attitude or a woeful outlook, which certainly doesn't lift anyone's spirits, least of all my own. I let hope fly out the window instead of latching on to it. Thank You for the reminder that hope is a precious commodity, one that gives me joy for the journey. More than anything, I want to be an example of biblical positivity no matter the weather. Today I choose to put my hope in You, Lord. Amen.

Day 2

GOD'S PLAN

My dear brothers and sisters, take note of this: Everyone should be quick to listen, slow to speak and slow to become angry.

JAMES 1:19 NIV

God gives good advice on anger. Often, if we listen carefully and hold our tongues, we don't become angry in the first place. Good communication forestalls a lot of emotional trauma. Hurt feelings often cause us to speak words we regret, simply making the problem worse. So when we feel tempted to react in anger, let's stop, listen, and hold our tongues for a while. That's God's plan for more peaceful relationships.

PRAYER

Lord, I've often heard it said that hurt people hurt people. That's definitely true. The times I've lashed out at others were usually times when I myself was hurting. I'm grateful for the reminder that I really can hold my tongue, even when I'm hurting. Especially when I'm hurting. It's not always easy, but it is possible with Your help. I don't want to be a tinder box, ready to explode at any moment. Those explosions never end well anyway. Guard my thoughts and my responses, no matter what I'm going through, I pray. Amen.

Day 3

WALKING BY FAITH

"Be strong and courageous, and act; do not fear nor be dismayed, for the LORD God, my God, is with you. He will not fail you nor forsake you."
1 CHRONICLES 28:20 NASB

What a life verse! What a creed to live by! We are assured that our God will never leave us or forsake us. We draw strength and courage from this assurance and are then able to act, to share our faith boldly and without fear because we are never alone. The Lord God—our God—is with us.

PRAYER

How many times have I allowed fear to cause me to freeze in place, Lord? Far too many to count! Calamity strikes and my feet suddenly feel like they're stuck in cement. My heart races. My hands tremble. I'm unable to take a step forward. I forget that You are with me. Then I read a verse like this and I'm reminded that no matter the situation—crisis or pain—I can be bold and courageous! When I realize You're right there, holding my hand, I'm strengthened from the inside out, knowing You'll never leave me. Amen.

Day 4

IN HIS HANDS

Do not be anxious about anything, but in every situation, by prayer and petition, with thanksgiving, present your requests to God.
PHILIPPIANS 4:6 NIV

Need a sure cure for anxiety? Start praying. As you trust that God has your best interests at heart, no matter what situation you face, His peace can replace concern. God says there's nothing you need to worry about. Just put all your troubles in His hands, and He who rules the universe yet knows each hair on your head will see that everything works out right. Are you ready to trust now?

PRAYER

Sometimes I cling tightly to things that were never mine to hold, Lord. I should release them to You, but instead I grip them like a dog with a bone. Anxiety creeps in and I wonder why I'm knotted up in fear. Then You remind me that I can pass those worries off to You. Your hands are big enough. And You have my best interests at heart. I can trust You to handle each situation in a way that will benefit me, not hurt me. Thank You for that! And thank You for knowing and loving me so beautifully! Amen.

Day 5

INTERIOR DECORATOR

You, Lord, are a shield around me,
my glory, and the One who lifts my head.
Psalm 3:3 NASB

Have you ever caught a glimpse of yourself reflected in a window and been shocked at the hangdog image you unwittingly portrayed? Slumped shoulders, drooping head, defeated expression? You can straighten your posture and adjust your face, but if the change doesn't come from the inside out, it won't stick. God is our interior decorator. Only He can provide that inner joy that projects outward and lifts our heads. Invite Him in to work on your place.

PRAYER

Okay, okay—I confess! I often walk around with slumped shoulders. I wear a defeated look on my face. There are days when I feel like I can't possibly lift my head or straighten my posture because it's just too hard. That's when You remind me that You are the lifter of my head, Lord! When I can't, You can! And You can flood my soul with joy, peace, patience, and all of the fruits of the Spirit I'm lacking. C'mon in and decorate this heart, Jesus! You are welcome here. Amen.

Day 6

GOD IS IN CONTROL

"Can any one of you by worrying add a single hour to your life?"
MATTHEW 6:27 NIV

What does worry gain us? It can't change the length of our days, except to diminish the health of our bodies. Ultimately, worry is the most self-defeating thing we can engage in. Besides, why should we give in to concern when God controls our lives? He will always set us on the right path, so we don't have to agonize over life's details.

PRAYER

I'll admit it, Lord: Sometimes I worry. I fret. I get twisted up with concern about the situations I'm facing. If worry could lengthen my days, I'd live to be a thousand! But the opposite seems to be true. Worry shortens my days. It interrupts my sleep. It causes me to make poor eating choices. It gives me headaches and ulcers. Ugh. Thank You for the reminder that worrying is a choice, one I can control. Today I choose not to worry. Instead, I give my concerns and fears to You, the one who knows me best and loves me most. Amen.

Day 7

DESIGNER LABEL

We wish each of you would always be eager to show how strong and lasting your hope really is.
HEBREWS 6:11 CEV

Our behavior is always on display, and like it or not, we are judged by our actions. . .and inactions. Without an explanation for our behavior—that we're motivated by our faith to be Christlike—people will come up with their own ideas: Her mama taught her right; she was just born nice; she acts sweet so everyone will like her. Isn't it better to be up front and give credit to the one we're emulating? Wear the label of your designer proudly.

PRAYER

I don't always wear Your label loudly or proudly, Lord. Sometimes I tuck it away in my pocket, choosing instead to show my temper. Or my irritation. Or my bitterness. I forget that the world is watching, that I'm supposed to be a reflection of You, my Creator. During those times, Lord, please give me one of those gentle nudges You're known for. Remind me that reflecting You is a better way to win people to the kingdom than allowing my behaviors to bring division and discord. I want to be a beacon of hope, a genuine reflection of my heavenly Father. Amen.

Day 8

BLESSING OTHERS

We work hard with our own hands. When we are cursed, we bless; when we are persecuted, we endure it.

1 CORINTHIANS 4:12 NIV

God gave Paul many blessings, and the apostle passed them on—even when the recipients didn't seem to deserve them. Those who cursed him (and they were many, no doubt) did not receive a cursing in return. Instead, Paul tried to bless them. Do we follow the apostle's example? When we are cursed by the words of others, what is our response?

PRAYER

I want to live out that old adage "Blessed to be a blessing," Lord. My heart's desire is to be a genuine blessing to others, even those who don't wish me well. It isn't always easy, especially when the hits keep coming from people I thought I could trust. But I know I look more like You when I'm blessing others. I'm more likely to draw people to Your Word when I actually obey it. And I have more peace in my heart when I extend blessings instead of curses. Thank You for that reminder today. Amen.

Day 9

INSIDE-OUT LOVE

God has made everything beautiful for its own time.
ECCLESIASTES 3:11 NLT

Beauty is a concern of every woman to some degree. We worry about hair, makeup, weight, fashions. . . But real beauty comes only from God's inside-out love. Once we're finally able to comprehend His infinite and extravagant love for us—despite our flat feet and split ends—our hearts will reflect radiant beauty from the inside out. Only when we feel truly loved are we free to be truly lovely.

PRAYER

The reflection in the mirror causes me pain sometimes, Lord. I don't like the face that stares back at me. The wrinkles. The worry lines. The age spots. Can this really be me? Then I'm reminded that Your idea of beauty is different from my own. You challenge me to live a life that's beautiful from the inside out, to understand that Your love makes me beautiful no matter how I think I look. May I love others extravagantly so that I can radiate Your beauty to all I come in contact with, Jesus. Amen.

Day 10

HOLD ON TO HOPE

The prospect of the righteous is joy,
but the hopes of the wicked come to nothing.
PROVERBS 10:28 NIV

Trusting in Jesus gave you new life and hope for eternity. So how do you respond when life becomes dark and dull? Does hope slip away? When no obviously great spiritual works are going on, don't assume God has deserted you. Hold on to Him even more firmly and trust that He will keep His promises. Truly, what other option do you have? Without Him, hope disappears.

PRAYER

Sometimes hope feels like a lifeline, Lord, one that I can choose to hang on to. . .or let go of. How many times have I released my hold, giving in to fear instead? (Way too many to count!) Today I choose to hold tight to You even when I feel like giving up. You are a God who keeps His promises. You're not letting go of me, so I won't let go of the hope You're giving me. My prospects are bright as long as I keep hanging on! Thanks for that reminder. Amen.

Day 11

GRANTER OF DREAMS

Hope deferred makes the heart sick,
but a dream fulfilled is a tree of life.
PROVERBS 13:12 NLT

As a teenager, I dreamed of writing a book one day. But life intervened, and I became a wife, mother, occupational therapist, and piano teacher. My writing dream was shelved. Twenty-five years later, after my youngest chick flew the coop, God's still, small voice whispered, "It's time." Within five years, the divine granter of dreams delivered more than seventy articles and nine book contracts. What is your dream? Be brave and take the first step.

PRAYER

I'm such a dreamer, Lord! There are so many things I want to do—with my life, my time, my gifts and talents. Thank You for awakening dreams in me in accordance with Your plans. I can count on You to make all of the arrangements, and I know I can always trust Your timing. So I won't fret when "my turn" seems late in coming. It will arrive at exactly the right moment. Until then, I continue to place my trust in You. Amen.

Day 12

A GODLY EXAMPLE

"Let the little children come to Me, and do not forbid them; for of such is the kingdom of heaven."
MATTHEW 19:14 NKJV

When He walked this earth, Jesus loved children. He never shut them out. Though their youth gave them little credence in Israel, He saw the faith potential in them. Certainly the children loved Jesus too for His kindheartedness. Do we shut children out of our lives because we are too busy or have more "important" things on our minds? If so, then we need to take an example from Jesus. For a new take on God's kingdom, spend time with a child today.

PRAYER

Jesus loves the little children. These are more than just lyrics, aren't they, Lord? You genuinely love them with Your whole heart. They mean the world to You and are worthy of Your very life. What's more, You want us to exhibit that same kind of love to the little ones in our path. Today, make me more sensitive to the children You've placed in my circle. May I be a light, an inspiration, a positive beacon of hope in this dark world. May children and grown-ups alike see in me a reflection of You. Amen.

Day 13

EVERYDAY BLESSINGS

But the eyes of the LORD are on those who fear him,
on those whose hope is in his unfailing love.
PSALM 33:18 NIV

The Lord of all creation is watching our every moment and wants to fill us with His joy. He often interrupts our lives with His blessings: butterflies dancing in sunbeams, dew-laced spiderwebs, cotton-candy clouds, and glorious crimson sunsets. The beauty of His creation reassures us of His unfailing love and fills us with hope. But it's up to us to take the time to notice.

PRAYER

How can I ever begin to thank You for the everyday blessings You've placed all around me, Lord? A toddler's giggles. A snow-capped mountaintop. A rushing river. A wriggling puppy's tail wagging in joy. Fluffy clouds in a bright blue sky. These and so many other miraculous blessings await me if only I will look! Today I ask that You open my eyes and my heart to the good gifts right in front me. May I see these things for what they truly are: miracles! Amen.

Day 14

GOD OF COMFORT

[God] comforts us in all our troubles,
so that we can comfort those in any trouble with
the comfort we ourselves receive from God.
2 CORINTHIANS 1:4 NIV

When you hurt, God offers you comfort. No trouble is so large or so small that He will not help. But after you have received His strength for the trouble at hand, do you share it in turn? Comfort isn't meant to be hidden away but rather passed on to those in similar need. As part of the body of Christ, we—the church—should be sharing the knowledge that God cares for and strengthens all His children.

PRAYER

You are the God of all comfort, Lord, and there have been so many times in my life when I've needed that comfort. In fact, there were moments when I felt sure I wouldn't make it. Then You intervened in Your gentle, loving way, calming the storm and bringing strength to these weary bones. I know I'm not promised a hurt-free life. That's a given. But knowing You're right there, and that You genuinely care, makes all the difference in the world. Thank You for loving me so well, my awesome Comforter! Amen.

Day 15

STOP THE ROLLER COASTER

Why am I discouraged? Why is my heart so sad? I will put my hope in God!

PSALM 43:5 NLT

For women, ruts of depression are often caused by careening hormones. Hormone fluctuations can cause us to spend countless hours weeping without knowing why—or to bite someone's head off, lose precious sleep, or sprout funky nervous habits. Knowing that this hormonally imbalanced state is only temporary, we must be intentional about placing our hope in God and praying that He will turn the downside up!

PRAYER

Sometimes I feel like my emotions truly are on a roller coaster, Lord. One day I'm up-up-up, and the next I go plummeting down. I know some of this is hormonal, but I'm also aware that You're bigger than all of that. You can settle me down, calm my nerves, and show me how to respond in ways that are honoring to You. Most of all, I can trust You to see me through every season of life, no matter how unpredictable, and keep me going with hope for a better tomorrow. I praise You even in the turmoil! Amen.

Day 16

LOOK TO THE SHEPHERD

The Lord is my shepherd, I lack nothing.
Psalm 23:1 NIV

Regardless of your physical circumstances, if Jesus is your shepherd, you never have to want spiritually. No matter what the world throws at you, you can be at peace. No fear overcomes those who follow the shepherd as their King. He guides them through every trial, leading them faithfully into an eternity with Him.

Are you lacking contentment today? Look to the shepherd for peace.

PRAYER

I think about the little sheep in the field, Lord. She's completely dependent on her shepherd. He guides her to food. To water. To shelter. To safety. He makes sure enemies are kept away. When she goes astray, he brings her back with his staff. In short, he's totally got her covered! It's the same with You. When I'm fretting, wondering how my needs will be met, where I'll live, what I'll do. . .You're right there—leading, guiding, and protecting. I love You, my precious shepherd! Amen.

Day 17

MY REFUGE

God is our refuge and strength,
always ready to help in times of trouble.
PSALM 46:1 NLT

What is your quiet place? The place you go to get away from the fray, to chill out, think, regroup, and gain perspective? Mine is a hammock nestled beneath a canopy of oaks in my backyard. . .nobody around but birds, squirrels, an occasional wasp, God, and me. There I can pour out my heart to the Lord, hear His voice comfort me, and feel His strength refresh me. We all need a quiet place. God, our refuge, will meet us there.

PRAYER

Life is noisy, Lord! There is chaos all around me. The TV blares. The children squabble. My boss spits out orders. My coworkers flit by intermittently, their chatter never-ending. And somehow, in the middle of it all, I'm supposed to find a quiet place? The only way I can discover such a sanctuary is to take the reins and make myself do it! Thank You for the reminder that it's not only possible; it's necessary for my well-being. Today I choose to draw myself away to a place of refuge where I can spend time with You, my comforter and my strength. Amen.

Day 18

WATCHFUL LOVE

I have learned in whatever state I am, to be content.

PHILIPPIANS 4:11 NKJV

Paul wasn't writing about a grit-your-teeth kind of contentment. He had learned to trust deeply in God for all his needs, so the apostle didn't worry about future events. His strength lay in God, who cared for his every need, even when churches forgot him.

We too can be content in Jesus. If the boss doesn't give us a raise or an unexpected bill comes in, He knows it. Nothing escapes His watchful love in our lives.

PRAYER

Lord, it's taking me awhile to understand this word *contentment*. Some days I think it's a feeling. Other days I think it's a state of mind, a choice. You want me to be content no matter what I'm going through—when I have little or when I have much. When I get my way and when I don't. Sounds like this is a moment-by-moment decision on my part, to choose to be content no matter what. It's going to take courage. So today I ask for just that—courage to be content regardless of what comes my way. Amen.

Day 19

STINKIN' THINKIN'

Let's be sober, having put on the breastplate of faith and love, and as a helmet, the hope of salvation.
1 THESSALONIANS 5:8 NASB

Women's hats aren't as popular as they once were, but you wouldn't know it by my closet. I love accessorizing with a perky hat to make a statement, to disguise a bad hair day, or to keep my brain from sautéing in the sizzling Florida sun. The Bible says we need to protect our minds from bad spiritual rays too. Nasty input produces nasty output: stinkin' thinkin'. When we're tempted to input a questionable movie or book, let's don our salvation helmets and say, "No way!"

PRAYER

Guarding my thoughts isn't always easy, Lord. Sometimes they ping around in my brain so fast I can't keep up with them! My imagination gets the best of me and terrifying thoughts compound, one on the other, until I've developed a scenario in my head that is so big and scary I can't seem to overcome it. That's when I'm reminded that I need to have Your thoughts, not my own. Today, Lord, fill my mind with truths from Your Word. No matter what I'm facing, I want Your perspective, not my own. So please guard my heart and my thoughts, I pray. Amen.

Day 20

OUR HOPE

God raised him from the dead, freeing him from the agony of death, because it was impossible for death to keep its hold on him.

ACTS 2:24 NIV

Death could not grasp Jesus, the sinless one who died for the guilty. Though death clings to sinful beings, it had no claim on God's Son. Jesus is our only hope. Though sin deserves death, God's compassion made a way to free us from its agonies. When we give our poor, mortal lives to Jesus, we rise in Him, sharing in His eternal life.

PRAYER

How amazing is this truth that the grave had no hold on You, Jesus! You conquered death, hell, and the grave. We humans worry about dying. Especially for nonbelievers, the thought of dying is unsettling, even terrifying. But for You? It didn't faze You one bit! You slipped right through death's slippery fingers. And thanks to the work You did on the cross, we can now escape eternal death as well. We've been freed from the agony of eternal separation from You because of Your sacrifice on the cross. How can we ever thank You enough for giving us eternal life? Our hearts are filled with gratitude! Amen.

Day 21

REDEMPTIVE PAIN

I may have fallen, but I will get up; I may be sitting in the dark, but the Lord *is my light.*
Micah 7:8 CEV

"Life is pain, Highness. Anyone who says differently is selling something." This memorable line from the movie *The Princess Bride* rings true. Pain is inevitable in life, but God can use it for redemptive purposes. Pain can knock us down, cast us into darkness, and make us feel defeated. But it's only as debilitating as we allow it to be. We will get up again; we will learn, adapt, and grow through redemptive pain.

PRAYER

Lord, I read in Your Word (Proverbs 24:16) that I might fall seven times but can still get back up again. This verse gives me hope because I seem to fall. . .a lot. I land in pits of darkness and despair more frequently than I'd like. I don't enjoy pain—I just want it to end quickly. And those feelings of defeat? I'm not a fan. But today I'm reminded that pain really is fleeting. There will be joy on the other side. I'll experience redemption for all those pits I've landed in. So thank You for holding me close as I traverse my way through the not-so-great stuff. I'm looking forward to the other side. Amen.

Day 22

GOD'S PROMISE

This is the promise that He has promised us—eternal life.

1 John 2:25 NKJV

The promise of eternal life comes straight from God. Those who receive Jesus into their hearts don't end their existence when they stop breathing. Their last breath on earth is merely the beginning of life in eternity with Jesus. Today you may be missing the one you lost, and your heart aches. But in eternity, you will be reunited and share the joys brought about by Jesus' victory over death. Until you meet again, simply trust in His unfailing promise.

PRAYER

Sometimes I think about the timeline of my life, Lord. It might have started with my physical birth, but it doesn't end with my physical death. From the moment I accepted You into my heart, the timeline shifted! I'm now walking out an eternal story, one with no end at all! I'm so grateful for the promise of heaven. I'm so excited about the prospect of seeing my loved ones again. And I'm thrilled to have Your perspective on life and death, an eternal perspective that overcomes every obstacle between my current situation and the bliss of heaven. Amen.

Day 23

MAID OF HONOR

For I fully expect and hope that. . .my life will bring honor to Christ, whether I live or die.
PHILIPPIANS 1:20 NLT

Honor. A word not as respected in our society as it once was. In these days of suggestive attire, cohabitation without marriage, and tolerance for every behavior imaginable, it's hard to remember what honor means. As Christians, our goal should be to honor Christ with our lives—especially in the details—because we are the only reflection of Jesus some people might ever see.

PRAYER

Lord, I want to honor You with my whole life—my words, my actions, my thoughts, and my demeanor. When people see my responses to life's challenges, may they see a reflection of You. I want to bring respect to Your holy and precious name. Help me be more aware of this goal in my day-to-day living. May I never forget that people are watching, especially those who know that I'm a Christian. I want to shine Your light brightly to draw others to You, not turn them away. That is the cry of my heart today. Amen.

Day 24

THE ONLY WAY

"I am the way and the truth and the life.
No one comes to the Father except through me."
JOHN 14:6 NIV

Plenty of people doubt Jesus. But those who have accepted Him as their Savior need not wallow in uncertainty. His Spirit speaks to ours moment by moment, if only we will listen. He tells us God has shown us the way; we need not seek another path or truth. No other road leads to God. For a vibrant Christian life, we simply need to continue down the path we're traveling with Jesus.

PRAYER

I've settled the issue in my heart, Jesus. You are the way, the truth, and the life. You're my way to the Father. You're my entrance to eternity. You're the key to love, joy, and peace in every situation. You're it. I don't need to keep looking—to other people, other things, other situations. All I ever need is found in You. Thank You for the reminder that all of the searching for satisfaction from what life has to offer will lead nowhere. In You I have absolutely everything I could ever need and more. How grateful I am! Amen.

Day 25

IT'LL BE ALL RIGHT

Our comfort is abundant through Christ.
2 CORINTHIANS 1:5 NASB

As children, we probably found great comfort in running to Mommy or Daddy and hearing, "It'll be all right." As adults, when we're frightened, dismayed, or dispirited, we yearn to run to enveloping arms for the same comfort. Abba Father—Papa God—is waiting with open arms to offer us loving comfort in our times of need. If we listen closely, we'll hear His still, small voice speak to our hearts: "It'll be all right, My child."

PRAYER

How many times have I run into Your arms over the years, Lord? A thousand? Ten thousand? I've needed Your comfort more times than I can count. That time my heart was broken. That time I was confused and needed direction. That time I was overcome with fear. Your arms were always wide enough. Your shoulders were always big enough. And Your embrace is always loving enough to woo me again, should I need it. So I lean in close today to hear Your still, small voice saying, "Come, child. Come." Amen.

Day 26

COMPASSION

Be merciful to those who doubt.

JUDE 1:22 NIV

If you've ever doubted (as we all have), you can understand why this verse is in the Bible. If well-meaning folks attacked you for your uncertainty, it probably didn't help—no doubt it just made you more nervous.

When questions enter our minds, we need someone encouraging to come alongside us and provide answers, not a critic who wants to condemn our feelings. Knowing that, we also need compassion for those who doubt. May we be the merciful ones who aid those doubting hearts.

PRAYER

I want to be the one who offers hope to the hopeless, Lord. May my words be the encouragement that lifts spirits and offers a ray of sunshine on an otherwise cloudy day. I don't ever want to be the Debbie Downer in the group. May the opposite be said of me! When people examine my life, may they say, "I could always count on her for a smile, a positive word, and a pat on the back." Those acts of compassion might seem small, but to the ones in need, such acts can be lifesaving. Show me who I can encourage today, I pray. Amen.

Day 27

I AM HIS

My health may fail, and my spirit may grow weak,
but God remains the strength of my heart; he is mine forever.
Psalm 73:26 NLT

My dear friend was dying of an inoperable brain tumor. Mother of three, forty-eight-year-old Sherill could no longer walk or care for herself, yet her voice was filled with hope as she gazed unwaveringly into my eyes and quoted this verse. She added something very significant at the end that I'll hold close to my heart and draw strength from when my time comes: "He is mine forever. . .and I am His."

PRAYER

Lord, there are days when I'm so weak I feel I can't go on. In my own strength, I cannot. But every time I mutter the words, "I can't!" You say, "I can!" During those seasons when my strength is fully depleted, I lean on You to do what I cannot. You lift me up. You lend me courage. You build my resolve. You offer hope. You give me eternal perspective to see beyond the weakness of today. So I place my trust in You to do all that I cannot. And I thank You in advance for loving me so well. Amen.

Day 28

ALWAYS SECURE

Your throne was established long ago; you are from all eternity.

PSALM 93:2 NIV

There was never a moment when God did not exist. No scrap of time or eternity came into being without Him, and nothing escapes His powerful reign. That's good news for His children. No matter what we face in this life, we know our Father is in control. No spiritual warfare or earthly disaster lies beyond His plan. No wickedness of Satan can take Him by surprise. Ours is the eternal Lord who has loved us from the start. In Him we are always secure.

PRAYER

Sometimes it's fun to think about eternity, Lord. I ponder Your eternal timeline and wonder what "forever" looks like from Your point of view. My finite mind cannot comprehend it, though I've certainly tried to figure it out. You always have been. You are. You always will be. And You've included me in this eternal story, offering me a chance to join You, not just now—while I'm walking this earth—but for all eternity. It's absolutely too much to comprehend, but I trust You, knowing You are in full control, Lord. You are our eternal God and we can trust You. . .always. Amen.

Day 29

INCREASING VISIBILITY

"Where then is my hope—who can see any hope for me?"
JOB 17:15 NIV

On hectic days when fatigue takes its toll, when we feel like cornless husks, hope fades. When hurting people hurt people and we're in the line of fire, hope flees. When our ideas fizzle, when our efforts fail, when we throw the spaghetti against the wall and nothing sticks, all hope can seem lost. But we must remember that this feeling is only temporary. The mountaintop isn't gone just because it's obscured by fog. Visibility will improve tomorrow and hope will rise.

PRAYER

It's one thing to lose my joy, Lord. It's another thing altogether to lose my hope. Hope is the great energizer. It bolsters my courage and gives me the "oomph" I need to keep going. Take that away and I wither on the vine. Thank You for the reminder that You are my hope, Jesus! I can't trust in anything—or anyone—else. Only You! Once I settle that issue in my mind, hope is restored. I can always keep my hope in You. You have never failed me, and You never will. Today I choose to place my trust in You. Amen.

Day 30

UNCHANGING

Your word, Lord, is eternal; it stands firm in the heavens.
Psalm 119:89 NIV

The Word of God never changes. The Father's commands do not change, and neither does Jesus, the Word made flesh, or His promise of salvation. Those who trust in Him are as secure as the Lord Himself, for He does not change, and none of His promises pass away unfulfilled. The eternal Lord and all of His commands stand firm. To gain eternity, simply receive Christ as your Savior; then trust in Him.

PRAYER

I feel like everything in my life is in a constant state of flux, Lord. My situations change. Relationships come and go. My emotions fluctuate. The weather shifts from hot to cold, wet to dry. My income bounces up and down. Yet somehow, in the middle of all of that, You remain steady. Firm. You don't change—in the day-to-day or from age to age. You are the same God who breathed life into Adam and the same one who decided to place me on this planet. I put my trust in You, my unchanging, all-knowing God! Amen.

Day 31

WAG MORE

I am not complaining about having too little.
I have learned to be satisfied with whatever I have.
PHILIPPIANS 4:11 CEV

I oozed envy as writer buddies received awards, broke sales records, and snagged lucrative contracts. What about me? Where were my accolades? It had always been enough to know I was following God's chosen path for me, but suddenly all I could do was complain. I wanted more.

Then God sent me a sign. Actually, it was a bumper sticker on a passing car: Wag More, Bark Less. Message received. . .with a smile.

PRAYER

I confess, Lord, that I often struggle with envy. I whine and complain when others receive blessings and I do not. I ask, "Why them? Why not me?" It's hard to keep things in perspective, to see the many ways I've already been blessed. Instead, I only see my lack. From now on I'm going to do my best to wag more and bark less. May I always express gratitude for the many ways in which You've already poured out Your blessings in my life. I'm forever grateful for Your generosity and want to show it with my whole heart. Amen.

Day 32

PURE DELIGHT

You make known to me the path of life; you will fill me with joy in your presence, with eternal pleasures at your right hand.

PSALM 16:11 NIV

Rejoicing in God? Those who don't know Jesus cannot imagine it. You have to know Jesus to delight in His presence, just as you cannot relish a friend until you come to know each other and enjoy companionship. But knowing and loving God brings us, His children, joy in His presence and the prospect of undefined pleasures at His side. Are you prepared to share those joys with Jesus for eternity?

PRAYER

In Your presence there is fullness of joy, Lord! Oh, I've experienced plenty of great times. Lots of laughs. Giddy responses to things like a baby's smile or a puppy's wagging tail. There have been many joyful moments with family and friends. But all of life's experiences—even the truly great ones—pale in comparison to the joy I'll experience in Your presence. And to think. . .I can go on experiencing these delights throughout eternity! What a good and generous heavenly Father You are to bestow such blessings on Your children! I'm so grateful. Amen.

Day 33

LORD OF THE DANCE

Remember your promise to me; it is my only hope.

PSALM 119:49 NLT

The Bible contains many promises from God: He will protect us (Proverbs 1:33), comfort us (2 Corinthians 1:5), help us in time of trouble (Psalm 46:1), and strengthen us (Isaiah 40:29). The word *encourage* comes from root words meaning "to inspire courage." Like an earthly father encouraging his daughter from backstage as her steps falter during her dance recital, our Papa God wants to inspire courage in us—if only we'll look to Him.

PRAYER

I've been on the receiving end of broken promises, Lord. If I'm being honest, I've even broken a few myself. It's easy to say, "I'll get back to you on that," and then walk away and forget. But You never forget. If You say You're going to do something, You follow through. I need to learn from Your example! Thank You for being a promise-keeping God. I'm so grateful You've always kept Your word and that You can be trusted. You always inspire courage in me! Amen.

Day 34

HE NEVER FAILS

If we are faithless, he remains faithful,
for he cannot disown himself.
2 TIMOTHY 2:13 NIV

Sometimes our faith fails, but Jesus never does. When we change for the worse, slip, or make a mistake, He is still the same faithful God He has always been. Though we may falter, He cannot. If we have given in to the tempter's wiles in some area of life, let us turn again to the Faithful One. If we have put our trust in Him, we can turn to Him for renewed forgiveness. His own faithfulness will not allow Him to deny us.

PRAYER

"I feel like such a failure." How many times have I spoken those words, Lord? The truth is, I mess up. . .a lot. I make mistakes. I have regrets. I wish I could push the rewind button and go back to before I created such a mess. But I can't. You, Lord? You never mess up! You're perfect and faithful in every way. You never have to ask for a redo. So today I put my trust in You, my perfect Father. Thank You for being so trustworthy, Lord. Amen.

Day 35

LIGHT MY FIRE

If God is for us, who can be against us?
ROMANS 8:31 NIV

Some days it feels as if the entire world is conspiring to make us as miserable as possible. Your spouse is crabby, the kids forgot to mention the four dozen cupcakes they volunteered you for today, traffic is terrible, your boss is on the rampage, your coworkers are in nasty moods, you forgot to defrost dinner, the car overheats again. But our God is King of the universe, and He's on our side. Girl, if that truth doesn't light your fire, the wood's wet.

PRAYER

You are for me. I needed to hear that today, Lord. I'll be honest—it often feels like everyone (and everything) is against me. The hits just keep coming. As I sit at the base of the ash heap, I feel lost. Confused. Alone. Then I'm reminded that You're right there next to me. Even if everything in my life falls apart, You won't crumble. If people turn on me, You will not. So today I take comfort in the fact that my heavenly Father is my number one advocate and friend! That brings me such joy! Amen.

Day 36

PERFECTION

His works are perfect, and all his ways are just.
A faithful God who does no wrong, upright and just is he.
DEUTERONOMY 32:4 NIV

Many unbelievers, or even weakening believers living in crisis, complain that God is unfair. But Moses, who suffered much for God's people, knew better than that. God is always perfect, faithful, and just—it's rebellious humanity that lacks these qualities.

We can have faith in God's perfection. He has never failed His people yet, though they have often been untrue. Trust in Him today. As He led His people to the promised land, He'll lead you home to Himself.

PRAYER

I don't always get it, Lord. Things happen that make no sense. I'm one of the ones who whines, "It's so unfair!" Please forgive me! Thank You for the reminder that Your ways are perfect. Even when they make no sense to me, I can trust Your plans for my life. So today I choose to rest easy in You. I won't fret. I won't point fingers. I won't feel sorry for myself. Instead, I'll just keep my eyes on the one who knows me best and loves me most. And I'll be sure to praise You, even when things make no sense. Amen.

Day 37

ACING THE TEST

Always be ready to give an answer when
someone asks you about your hope.
1 PETER 3:15 CEV

Remember algebra tests in high school? Instant sweat and heart palpitations. You dreaded going into them unprepared. You wanted to have answers ready so you wouldn't be left with saliva drooling from your gaping mouth when questioned. The Bible says we should be prepared when someone asks about the hope within us—the hope they couldn't help but notice radiating from our souls. The answer scores an A+ for all eternity: Jesus!

PRAYER

I don't always pass the tests life sends my way, Lord. Sometimes I get the answers wrong (and in a spectacularly public way—ugh!). Thank You for the reminder that I'm still on a learning curve. I'm not perfect and I don't always get it right, but I do want to keep growing in my faith and in my knowledge of Your Word. When people ask me, "Where does your hope come from?" may I be ready with a quick answer: "From my relationship with Jesus, of course!" May I live a life that draws people to You, Lord. Amen.

Day 38

PRAISE HIM

Let them praise the name of the Lord, for His name alone is exalted; His glory is above the earth and heaven.

Psalm 148:13 NKJV

Trusting Jesus gives you a spectacular view of God's power. His work in your life increasingly opens your eyes to this glorious King who loves you. But those who don't know Him cannot praise Him. They are thoroughly blind to the splendor of the one whom they have denied. Yet in the end, His glory will be apparent even to them. Whom do you follow—the glorious one or mere humans?

PRAYER

Praise is a powerful weapon, Lord. I use it often! Sometimes it makes me sad that friends don't seem to understand, but that's because many don't know You like I do. If they did, they would be praising too! I've been a witness to so many miracles over the years. So many near misses. So many second chances. I've seen Your goodness, both in my own life and in the lives of those around me. Because You have proven Yourself time and time again, I have so much to praise You for! Thank You, my all-knowing God! Amen.

Day 39

CHEF D'OEUVRE

Be strong and let your heart take courage,
all you who wait for the Lord.
Psalm 31:24 NASB

Identical eggs can be turned into greasy fried egg sandwiches or an exquisite soufflé. The difference is how much beating they endure.

When life seems to be beating us down, we must remember that we are masterpieces in progress. The slicing, dicing, and mixing may feel brutal at times, but our Lord has offered us His courage and strength to endure until He is ready to unveil His chef d'oeuvre.

PRAYER

I often feel beaten down, Lord. Life has been hard on me, and people aren't always kind. Honestly? Situations aren't always kind either. Some days they stink! I want to respond well to the not-so-great days, but I don't always do so. My attitude sours or I get swallowed up in defeat. Thank You for the reminder that I don't always have to get it right. I might be a greasy egg sandwich today and a beautiful soufflé tomorrow. Show me how to deal with the egg sandwich days so I don't get bogged down and discouraged.

Day 40

BUILDING A HOUSE

The wise woman builds her house,
but the foolish pulls it down with her hands.
PROVERBS 14:1 NKJV

Did you know you can build a house? God says so. No, you won't use mortar, brick, and wood. But every Christian woman has the ability to build up her family with her wisdom, industry, and righteousness. Her faithful Christian character blesses those in her home. Today, are you building your house or tearing it down? Seek God, and He will help you make it strong.

PRAYER

Building is hard work, Lord. It's wearying. As a woman, I do my best to build, build, build. . .my family, my friends, my coworkers, my fellow congregants at my church. I try to bless others and help them grow. I don't always get it right. There are days when my words aren't edifying. They're laced with anger and frustration. Still, I do my best to keep going—day in and day out. Thank You for reminding me that my words matter. My actions matter. The way I treat others—both in and out of my household—matters, to them and to You. Amen.

Day 41

SUPERGLUE FAITH

In Him, you also, after listening to the message of truth, the gospel of your salvation—having also believed, you were sealed in Him with the Holy Spirit of the promise.

EPHESIANS 1:13 NASB

Remember the old commercial that depicted a construction worker dangling in midair, the top of his helmet bonded by superglue to a horizontal beam? Faith is like superglue. We cling to our God, our foundation, our beam. As believers, we are sealed in Christ, and the bond cannot be undone. Through prayer in times of despair, our faith is strengthened and becomes waterproof, pressure-resistant, and unbreakable.

PRAYER

I love the idea that I'm sealed to You, Lord. I can't think of anyone else I'd rather be sealed to! There are times when I feel like I'm barely hanging on, but You never let go of me. We truly have an unbreakable bond, You and me. I'm sealed in Christ—not just now but for all eternity! Why would I ever want to walk away, anyway? Life apart from You would be lonely, dangerous, and riddled with complications. So I'll stick with You. And I thank You for loving me enough to want to be eternally bonded! Amen.

Day 42

PARENTS

"Honor your father and your mother,
that your days may be long upon the land."
EXODUS 20:12 NKJV

When we honor our parents, we may not spend much time in the promised land, but God will bless us. Treating Mom and Dad well improves our relationships with them and gives our family security. As we treat our children's grandparents well, we model the actions of adult children, and our children are more likely to treat us well too.

Our Father God has special blessings for those of us who respect our parents. Whether it's Holy Land property or deeper love, He gives us just what we need.

PRAYER

This is one of the few commands that comes with a promise, and I love it! If I do this (respect my parents), You'll do that (lengthen my days). It's so wonderful to live in a family where we see this kind of respect. May I always convey such love and honor—not just to my actual parents but to all of the elderly people You place in my path. They are truly valuable on so many levels and worthy of my admiration and respect. One day I'll be an elderly person and I'll want to reap kindness and respect—so I'll sow them now. Amen.

Day 43

KEEP BREATHING, SISTER!

As long as we are alive, we still have hope,
just as a live dog is better off than a dead lion.
ECCLESIASTES 9:4 CEV

Isn't this a tremendous scripture? At first glance, the ending elicits a chuckle. But consider the truth it contains: Regardless of how powerful, regal, or intimidating a lion is, when he's dead, he's dead. But the living—you and I—still have hope. Limitless possibilities! Hope for today and for the future. Although we may be like lowly dogs, fresh, juicy bones abound. As long as we're breathing, it's not too late!

PRAYER

As long as there is life, there is hope. How I love these words, Lord! Hope is such a precious commodity. I confess, I often give up too easily. I face an overwhelming problem and give in to defeat. My hope flies out the window. But this verse reminds me that no matter what I face, I can keep going as long as there is breath in my lungs. So from now on, never let me forget that my future is filled with possibilities. I have nothing to fear, nothing to worry about. There is plenty of hope ahead for me! Amen.

Day 44

APPRECIATION FOR MOTHERS

Her children arise and call her blessed;
her husband also, and he praises her.
PROVERBS 31:28 NIV

Wouldn't every woman like to receive this kind of praise? A few do. Yet, though we all need praise for a job well done, many families forget to encourage their members. When we have followed God faithfully, it shows in our lives, but we still value others' appreciation. Has a Christian mother been a wonderful influence on your life? She'd probably like to know that. Feel free to share that praise with others too.

PRAYER

What a wonderful reminder to praise the mothers in our lives, Lord! Sometimes we overlook them. We don't realize the work they do on our behalf. But today I will take the time to bless a mom—either my own or someone else's. Give me creative ideas. Should I deliver flowers? Bake cookies? Write a note of encouragement? Offer to help her with housework or laundry? I want to be a blessing and ease the pressure. She's worth it, Lord! You love moms. . .and so do I. Thank You for the reminder that I should treat them with care. Amen.

Day 45

IT'S A MYSTERY

This is the day which the Lord *has made;*
let's rejoice and be glad in it.
Psalm 118:24 NASB

Let's face it, girls, some mornings our rejoicing lasts only until the toothpaste drips onto our new shirt or the toast sets off the fire alarm. But the mystery of Jesus-joy is that it's not dependent on rosy circumstances. If we, after cleaning the shirt and scraping the toast, intentionally give our day to the Lord, He will infuse it with His joy. Things look much better through Jesus-joy contact lenses!

PRAYER

I don't always find joy in every situation, Lord. Sometimes life's circumstances zap it away in an instant, before I even know what has hit me. But when I remember that Your joy is my strength, I get excited all over again. And the best part is, I don't have to drum it up. It's not dependent on my emotions. You pour it out, usually when I least expect it. So today I open my hands and heart to You. Fill me up, I pray! Give me the joy-joy-joy so that I can rejoice no matter what life throws my way! Amen.

Day 46

FEAR WILL FLEE

Do not be afraid of sudden terror, nor of trouble from the wicked when it comes; for the Lord *will be your confidence, and will keep your foot from being caught.*

Proverbs 3:25–26 NKJV

What do you have to fear, with God as your confidence? He protects you from being snared like a wild animal by the world's troubles. With His hand over you, no sudden event or evildoer's plot can destroy you. Give Him your full trust, and fear will flee.

PRAYER

Sometimes it's hard not to panic, Lord. Situations hit from out of the blue and I'm blindsided. My hands start shaking. My knees start knocking. I slip into what I sometimes call the white zone. In that space, I'm driven forward by the emotion of the moment. You say I don't have to live this way. You can keep my foot from being caught when these crises hit. So today I choose to put my trust in You. Thank You for the reminder that no sudden event or evil will overtake me. With You on my side, I'm going to make it through every crisis that comes. (Have I mentioned how grateful I am for that?) Amen.

Day 47

GOING THE DISTANCE

[David]. . .chose five smooth stones from the stream. . .and, with his sling in his hand, approached the Philistine.

1 SAMUEL 17:40 NIV

The young man David had no intention of backing down from his fight. Notice he picked up five rocks, not just one. He was prepared to go the distance against his giant. He fully expected God to make him victorious, but he knew it wouldn't be easy.

So you've used your first rock against your giant. Maybe even your second. But don't give up. Keep reloading your sling and go the distance. Victory is sweet!

PRAYER

I'm feeling discouraged today, Lord. I've been slinging my stones for a while now and the giant keeps taunting me from the other side of the field. But I won't give up, even if he doesn't drop to the ground as quickly as I would like. Give me the passion and courage of young David to keep going even when the odds seem stacked against me. I don't want to go down in history as one who gave up. May I go the distance, no matter how long it takes. And may I honor You every step of the way. Amen.

Day 48

FEARING GOD

In the fear of the Lord there is strong confidence,
and His children will have a place of refuge.
Proverbs 14:26 NKJV

There is only one right kind of fear: the fear of God. Not that we need to cower before Him, but we must respect and honor Him and His infinite power. Those who love Him also rightly fear Him. But those who fear God need fear nothing else. He is their refuge, the protector whom nothing can bypass. Fear God, and you are safe.

PRAYER

I remember wondering as a child what it meant to "fear" You, Lord. I used to wonder if my knees should knock when I prayed to You! Now I get it. To "fear" You is to treat You with complete reverence. You are worthy of honor and praise, far above all others. You are the creator and author of all! It's hard to watch the world completely ignore or blaspheme You. These lost souls have no idea what they're doing. But for those of us who love You? We have nothing to fear. We are promised protection and love no matter what the world throws our way. Amen.

Day 49

TOP OFF MY TANK

"My grace is sufficient for you, for my power is made perfect in weakness."
2 CORINTHIANS 12:9 NIV

There is no weaker vessel than a bedraggled mother at 6:00 a.m. staring into the bathroom mirror after another rough night. She's trying to decide if the dark smudges beneath her eyes are yesterday's grape jelly when she suddenly realizes she's brushing her hair with her toothbrush. Yep, we are a sisterhood of slightly sagging spiritual warriors, but we can depend on God to power our weak vessels. He is able.

PRAYER

I've been at that point, Lord, where I feel so weak I wonder how I can manage to face another day. The image staring back at me in the mirror looks haggard. Tired. Defeated. I definitely don't feel up for the fight. Then, just like that, You infuse me with power from on high. Your Holy Spirit fills me, giving me courage, strength, power, and joy. I never could have come up with these things on my own, but You're suddenly filling my proverbial tank with everything I need. Thank You for being my strength when I am weak. Amen.

Day 50

SECURE IN THE FATHER

The Spirit you received does not make you slaves, so that you live in fear again; rather, the Spirit you received brought about your adoption to sonship. And by him we cry, "Abba, Father."

ROMANS 8:15 NIV

As part of God's family, you need never dread anything. He who rules the universe adopted you. Since your loving Father no longer condemns you for your sin, panic need not rule your life. Fear no retribution, because your elder brother, Jesus, shed His blood for you, covering every transgression. God's child always remains secure in her Abba Father.

PRAYER

Sometimes fear comes over me like a dark cloud, Lord. One minute, bright shiny skies. The next? Storm clouds hover, causing everything to go dark. It's not always easy to keep my peace. Sometimes, when the darkness envelops me, I find myself curled up in a ball, terrified. Then I remember that I'm Your child. You're my Abba, my Daddy. And You are right there ready to draw me into Your arms and remind me that I'm never alone, that I can trust You. No matter what I face, Abba, I can rest safe in Your arms! Amen.

Day 51

HEAVYWEIGHT

This hope is like a firm and steady anchor for our souls.

HEBREWS 6:19 CEV

Julia and Mark anchored their sailboat to do a little reef exploring while they went diving. When they surfaced, the boat was a speck on the horizon. It had drifted more than a half mile because their anchor was too light.

Hope in Christ is an anchor for our souls. But if the anchor isn't weighted by firm and steady faith, we may drift in strong currents of doubt, problems, or disillusionment. Weigh your anchor today.

PRAYER

There are days when I don't anchor myself to You, Lord. I get busy. I forget. I take off swimming, chasing after my own plans, my own dreams, and then realize You seem far away. It's not always easy to acknowledge that You're not the one who has drifted. I have. It's all on me. Today I choose to link arms with You, to stay rooted and grounded. No matter what I'm facing, I will stay afloat as long as I stay anchored to You. Currents may come and go, but I will remain steady with my hand planted firmly in Yours. Amen.

Day 52

THE BLESSING OF FORGIVENESS

[Our] sins have been forgiven on account of his name.

1 JOHN 2:12 NIV

Who could do something wonderful enough to earn God's forgiveness? No human work can buy it. God forgives because of who He is, not because of who we are or what we do. It's encouraging to realize we can't earn forgiveness by our own perfection. Instead, forgiveness becomes the great blessing of our Christian life that makes living for Jesus possible. We obey God to show our appreciation, not to gain entry into His kingdom.

PRAYER

There are times when I wish I had a lot of money, Lord. It would be fun to go to the store and buy anything I wanted—for myself or for others. Instead, I pinch pennies. I shop at less expensive stores. . .on purpose. When I think about how lavishly You've poured out forgiveness on us, I'm so grateful! Even if I had a million dollars, I couldn't buy it. Instead, You offered it for free when Your Son, Jesus, went to the cross for me. How can I ever thank You enough for Your generosity? Amen.

Day 53

A PERFECT FIT

The Lord is good to those whose hope is in him, to the one who seeks him.
Lamentations 3:25 NIV

Seeking God is, for some, like a child groping in a dark room for the light switch. She knows it's there; she just can't seem to put her fingers on it. Some search for God all their lives, trying on various religions like pairs of shoes. This one pinches. That one chafes. But we must bypass religious fluff for the heart of the matter: Jesus. The only way to God is through faith in Christ (John 14:6). Suddenly, the shoe fits!

PRAYER

I love the promise found in Your Word, Lord, that if I seek You I will surely find You. I've spent a good portion of my life searching—though at times I wasn't sure what (or who) I was searching for. Then, suddenly, there You were! You appeared at the perfect moment, ready to sweep in and take the reins of my life, to relieve me of my past, my guilt, and my shame. Now my searching days are over! I've settled in with You, not just for the rest of this life but for all eternity. How grateful I am! Amen.

Day 54

AN END TO MOURNING

"Blessed are those who mourn, for they will be comforted."
MATTHEW 5:4 NIV

How often do we think of mourning as a good thing? But when it comes to sin, it is. Those who grieve their own sinfulness will turn to God for forgiveness. When He willingly responds to their repentance, mourning ends. Comforted by God's pardon, transformed sinners celebrate—and joyous love for Jesus replaces sorrow.

PRAYER

You bring comfort to the mourner, Lord. I know, because I've experienced Your comfort in my own life. There have been seasons when the grief was so palpable, so excruciating, that I didn't think I would ever get past it. Then somehow, in that tender, loving way of Yours, You drew near and comforted me. You eased me through it. Your very presence gave me the courage I needed to keep going. I've even mourned during seasons of rebellion, only to see You come close and offer forgiveness. What a gracious Father You are! Amen.

Day 55

ROOTS

"There is hope for your future," declares the LORD, *"and your children will return to their own territory."*
JEREMIAH 31:17 NASB

Prodigal. The word alone evokes an involuntary shudder.

Most of us know parents whose children have left home in the throes of rebellion. Some of us are those parents. After years of protecting and nurturing our children, we're stunned when heartache replaces harmony, panic supersedes pride. But the Great Peacemaker declares that prodigals will one day return to their roots. One of His greatest parables reinforces that hope (Luke 15).

PRAYER

Oh, how I love this promise that prodigals will one day return home, Lord! I've witnessed it in my own life. I've often wandered away from You, only to be drawn back time and time again. Even in my most rebellious state, I've felt Your gentle tug on my heart! No one else can draw me back like You can. Today I pause to pray for all of the prodigals in my life. Begin to woo them in that remarkable way You have, Father. Draw them back to the fold. Until then, I will remain hopeful. May everyone come to know You as Father and friend! Amen.

Day 56

CHOSEN FAMILY

There is a friend that sticketh closer than a brother.
PROVERBS 18:24 KJV

Family relationships range from the wonderful to the disturbing, and we get whatever God gives us. But we choose our friends based on common interests and experiences. Often this "chosen family" seems closer to us than siblings. Yet neither clings closer than our elder brother, Jesus. He teaches us how to love blood relatives and those we choose. Regardless of whether we're related, when we love each other in Him, that love sticks fast.

PRAYER

Have I paused lately to thank You for my friends, Lord? I'm so blessed to be surrounded by people who love me. . .and love You. I've chosen the friends in my inner circle with care. They build me up. They make me laugh. And they love me enough to let me know when I'm off track. We have that kind of relationship. Our bond is almost closer than family at times, honestly. They stick as close as a brother or sister ever would. Thank You for giving me just the right people for this leg of my journey. Amen.

Day 57

A LEGACY OF LOVE

After all, when the Lord Jesus appears, who else but you will give us hope and joy and be like a glorious crown for us?
1 THESSALONIANS 2:19 CEV

The most hope-inspiring legacy we can pass on to the next generation is faith. What a delight it is for us as women to plant and nurture seeds of faith in our children, knowing that at harvest they'll stand by our sides before the Lord Jesus! It's never too late to till the fertile soil of their hearts through our example of daily Bible reading, prayer, and dependence on our Savior.

PRAYER

This is my prayer, Lord, that I might leave a legacy of faith when I'm gone. May people say of me, "She loved Jesus and showed others how to embrace a life with Him." Especially as I ponder the seeds of faith I'm planting in my children, but also as I contemplate every nonbelieving adult I know and love, I long for my example to make a difference. May each one see my faith and be drawn to it. . .and to You. A harvest is coming, Lord! I can feel it and I'm so excited! Amen.

Day 58

PRAYERFUL GIVING

Give, and it shall be given unto you;
good measure, pressed down. . .and running over.
LUKE 6:38 KJV

Need an example of how to give? Look to God. To those who give generously, He gives abundant, overflowing blessings.

In this fallen world, we need to be careful about the people and organizations we choose to support financially. Dishonest people or those who oppose God should not receive our charitable gifts. But many Christian ministries do good work and need our support. Faithful churches need our giving. As we donate prayerfully, God will bless us in return.

PRAYER

It feels so good to help out, and I want to give with a cheerful heart, Lord. That's why I'm so diligent to search out individuals and organizations doing reputable work so that I can contribute to the cause. Thank You for giving me discernment so that my money can be spent wisely. I want to make a difference in this world, and I know that accountability plays a role. Thank You for making me aware of so many wonderful ministries and charities I can help. Together, we can accomplish much in Your name! Amen.

Day 59

HIS LITTLE GIRLS

Just as a father has compassion on his children,
so the LORD *has compassion on those who fear Him.*
PSALM 103:13 NASB

Plagued with horrible recurring nightmares during my childhood, I remember the terror of waking up screaming, hair sweat-plastered to my face. Then, like a candle in the darkness, my father would appear at my bedside, lie beside me, and gently rub my back until I fell asleep. Our heavenly Father is like that—tender, caring, protective. And He too responds when His little girls need the comfort of His loving presence.

PRAYER

How many times have I felt Your presence when I needed it most, Lord? During those horrible hours when I watched loved ones suffer. During those seasons when I felt completely alone. During those complicated moments when my heart seemed to betray me. There You were, right there, always loving, always caring, always comforting. Your compassion somehow made its way to my heart, breaking through the darkness and bringing hope. You are truly my Abba Father, the one who protects, guides, and loves as no one else can. I'm so grateful for Your tender presence in my life, Lord! Amen.

Day 60

WANT VERSUS NEED

"Give us this day our daily bread."
MATTHEW 6:11 NKJV

Jesus tells us here to ask God for our daily needs, and we may do that frequently. Let's remember that even the smallest things, such as the bread we put on the table, come from God. Yet have we forgotten that all our food comes from our heavenly Father? God forgets nothing we need. So if we don't have steak instead of hamburgers, could it be because we *want* but don't *need* it?

PRAYER

Sometimes I find myself getting worked up and worried, Lord. Usually, if I'm being honest, it's because I've taken my eyes off You. I've forgotten to trust You. Thank You for the reminder that I have to be diligent in fixing my eyes on You. All things come from You, so I need to focus on You, my source. It's not my job (though that's great). It's not my bank balance (though it is often a reflection of what You're doing in my life). Truly, You are my source, so I will look to You, my perfect provider! Amen.

Day 61

LET THE SUN SHINE IN

"Come to me, all you who are weary and burdened, and I will give you rest."

MATTHEW 11:28 NIV

Nothing chokes hope like weariness. Day in and day out, drudgery produces weariness of body, heart, and soul. It feels like dark clouds have obscured the sun and cast us into perpetual shadow. But Jesus promised rest for our weary souls, respite from our burdens, and healing for our wounds. . .if we come to Him. The sun isn't really gone; it's just hidden until the clouds roll away.

PRAYER

Sometimes it feels like the sun is hidden away, Lord. Evening's shadows fall at unexpected times and I feel swallowed up in exhaustion. There are times when the weariness is so extreme I feel like I literally can't move. I'm glued to the sofa. Or the bed. My "want to" evaporates, along with my energy. During those seasons I often push through, but You are teaching me that it's better to hit the pause button and get some much-needed rest. I'll be no good to anyone if I don't refresh and restore my weary soul. Thank You for that reminder. Amen.

Day 62

SHARE HIS LOVE

"It is more blessed to give than to receive."
ACTS 20:35 NIV

Christmas has become a time of receiving—to the point where greed motivates more people than blessing. But Paul reminds us that getting what we want is not the greatest blessing. We know that when we see the delight in a child's eyes at receiving a longed-for item. Our heavenly Father loves to see the same joy in our eyes when He helps us in less tangible ways. That's why He tells us to share His love with others.

PRAYER

Giving is pure delight, Lord! I can hardly wait to bless others. Sometimes I plan and strategize special gifts for my loved ones, hoping to bring great joy. Sure, it's fun to receive too, but I'm always tickled to give. There's something about seeing the excitement in a grandchild's eyes or the smile on a coworker's face that makes it worth any amount of sacrifice. You must feel this way about blessing Your kids too—surely You experience great joy in pouring Yourself out on our behalf. (We've learned from the best, Lord!) Amen.

Day 63

NO WIMPS HERE

For God has not given us a spirit of fear and timidity, but of power, love, and self-discipline.

2 TIMOTHY 1:7 NLT

Do you suffer paralysis by analysis? Are you so afraid of trying something new that you put it off until you can think it through. . .and end up doing nothing at all? Too much introspection creates inertia, and we abhor the ineffective wimps we become. Sisters, God never intended for us to be wimps. His power and love are available to replace our fear and infuse us with courage. Shake off that paralysis and get moving!

PRAYER

Inertia is a real problem at times, Lord. I find myself frozen in place, unable to make a decision. Unable to take a step. Fear wriggles its way down my spine and literally paralyzes me. My thoughts take over, playing in full technicolor. They hold me captive, like a spectator in a movie theater. Somehow I become convinced there's no fight left in me. That's when I'm reminded that You fight my battles, Lord! What I cannot do, You can. . .and will! So today I choose to shake off my inertia and dive back into the battle, no matter how tense! Amen.

Day 64

THE FATHER'S COMPASSION

A father to the fatherless, a defender of widows, is God in his holy dwelling.
PSALM 68:5 NIV

God's love is very tender toward those who hurt. Children who have lost their fathers and women who have lost their husbands can count on His compassion. When we lose a loved one, do we focus on the Father's gentleness? We may be more likely to complain that He didn't extend life than to praise Him for His care. But when we feel the most pain, we also receive the largest portion of God's comfort. What hurts His children hurts Him too.

PRAYER

The world seems harsh at times, Lord. People can be so rude as they rush by us on their way here and there. And often even those who love us most don't seem to notice when we're hurting. So we suffer in silence. We wonder if anyone cares. If they did, would they slow down long enough to engage us? Then we're reminded that You always care. You know every ache. You feel every pain. And Your compassion is genuine. You sweep in and comfort us as only You can. Thank You, my defender, my protector, for loving me so well! Amen.

Day 65

WHEN I'M BAAAD

"I am the good shepherd; I know my own sheep, and they know me, just as my Father knows me and I know the Father."

JOHN 10:14–15 NLT

Ever spent much time around sheep? They're self-centered creatures. All they think about is eating, sleeping, and avoiding conflict. But one good thing about sheep is that they'll drop everything in response to their shepherd's voice. Not anybody else's voice, just the familiar tones of their own shepherd. This little ewe wants to recognize and respond to her beloved shepherd's voice too. How about you, ewe?

PRAYER

Sometimes the voices around me are so loud, so consuming, that I almost miss Yours, Lord. I have to pull away, to quiet myself, in order to hear Your still, small voice. I have a long way to go when it comes to responding to Your voice. There are times—naughty little sheep that I am—when I deliberately tune You out. But knowing and responding to Your voice is key to my life's success rate. So I'll do my best to lean in closer and hear—then follow—all You say. Amen.

Day 66

SIMPLE WORDS

Strengthen those who have tired hands,
and encourage those who have weak knees.
ISAIAH 35:3 NLT

A simple word of encouragement or act of kindness can live in memory for years and even a lifetime. You may think someone who holds a high position or appears to have everything under control doesn't need any encouragement, but you never know how unsure of herself or emotionally frayed she's feeling inside. Perhaps your "Wonderful job!" is the confidence booster she's longing to hear. It's possible your thumbs-up is all it will take for someone to know that others notice, understand, and care.

PRAYER

Sometimes, when I'm talking about a good friend, I'll say, "She's such a good person." And many of my friends are good people, Lord. (You did a fantastic job with them, for sure!) But as good as we may be, humans will never come close to the kind of goodness You convey to Your kids. You're tender. Compassionate. Genuine. You never tire of caring for us, especially when we're hurting. And if I'm being honest, life is hard. I hurt. . .a lot. Still, You're there every time, ready to fold me into Your arms and wash all of my worries away. I'm so grateful! Amen.

Day 67

TOLERANCE ISN'T ENOUGH

"In his name the nations will put their hope."
MATTHEW 12:21 NIV

In the summer of 2000, my husband and I toured the Holy Land. Our Israeli guide assured us that there was no safer place than Jerusalem, because people of numerous faiths—Muslim, Jewish, Christian, Hindu—had learned tolerance as the key to living together peaceably. Yet tension was as evident as the armed guards on every street corner. Violence erupted three months later with the first bus bombings of the Second Intifada. Our only hope for peace is Jehovah.

PRAYER

I'm reminded today, Lord, that You are the Prince of Peace. I can't look to any political leaders to bring about world peace (or even peace in my nation or state). Only You can bring about the kind of peace that transforms lives and changes situations long-term. So no matter how things look in the natural, I won't be shaken. World events won't rock me or determine my outlook. Instead, I'll continue to look to You and You alone. You are my only hope, Jesus! May I never forget that. Amen.

Day 68

CHILDREN OF GOD

Because you are his sons, God sent the Spirit of his Son into our hearts, the Spirit who calls out, "Abba, Father."
GALATIANS 4:6 NIV

God draws His children near, connecting them firmly to Himself through the Son and the Holy Spirit. There is no division in the Godhead when it comes to loving God's adopted children. With the Spirit, we call out, "Abba, Daddy," to the Holy One who loved us enough to call us to Himself despite our sin. Through Jesus' sacrifice and the Spirit's work, God the Father cleanses us and reconciles us to Himself, empowering us to follow Him day by day.

PRAYER

You welcome me, Abba Father, in spite of my many flaws and weaknesses. You say, "Come to Me, child," and sweep me into Your arms, even on my toughest days. You're not keeping track of my mess-ups (thank goodness) and You would never reject me. I'm learning from You how to treat others. I want to love them this same way, to connect with them as brothers and sisters, all children of our precious and loving heavenly Father. Thanks for the reminder that we're all adopted into one big family. Amen.

Day 69

QUESTIONS AND ANSWERS

And the Scriptures were written to teach and encourage us by giving us hope.
ROMANS 15:4 CEV

What do you do when facing a perplexing problem? Ask a family member? Consult a friend? Turn to the internet?

God's Word is brimming with answers to life's difficulties, yet it's often the last place we turn. God still speaks to us today through the lives of trusting Abraham, brokenhearted Ruth, runaway Jonah, courageous Esther, female leader Deborah in a male-dominated society, beaten-down Job, double-crossing Peter, and "worst of sinners" Paul, who proved people can change.

PRAYER

I feel like I'm always looking for answers, Lord. On the internet. From my friends. From the spiritual leaders at my church. Whenever I have a problem or I'm facing a tough challenge, I run to get "the answer" as quickly as I can. But the world doesn't often have the answers I need to my problems. So I'm grateful for the reminder that You are the answer. You're continually speaking to my heart and will give me wisdom to know what to do and when to do it. Thank You for always leading and guiding, Lord. Amen.

Day 70

STAND FIRM

The Lord has become my fortress,
and my God the rock in whom I take refuge.
Psalm 94:22 NIV

Are you under attack by friends, family, or coworkers? If it comes because of your obedience to the Lord, stand firm in the face of their comments. He will defend you. If you encounter harsh words or nasty attitudes, remain kind, and He will assist you. Should your boss do you wrong, don't worry. Those who are against a faithful Christian are also against God, and He will somehow make things right.

PRAYER

Sometimes the attacks come with such vengeance that I can barely hold on, Lord. I feel my knees buckling out from under me and my "want to" waning. Giving up seems easier than persisting. Then I'm reminded that You've called me to stand firm no matter what. So today I choose to do that. I will picture myself as a triumphant warrior, arms raised, seeing the battle as already won. . .because it is. I will take refuge in You, knowing I'm already victorious thanks to You. I'm grateful for that reminder. Amen.

Day 71

HIT THE MATS

Blessed are those whose help is the God of Jacob,
whose hope is in the LORD their God.
PSALM 146:5 NIV

Wrestled with God lately? We all do at one time or another. The Genesis 32 account of Jacob's wrestling match with the Almighty reassures us that God is not offended when we beat on His chest and shout, "Why?" He understands that we sometimes have to wrestle out the mysteries of our faith. Wrestling with his Lord was a turning point for Jacob—he got a new name (Israel) and a new perspective. God is ready to do the same for us.

PRAYER

There are times when I feel it's irreverent to argue with You, Lord. But there are other times when I come out swinging. Life is unfair and I don't understand what's happening. So I come to You, hands curled into fists, ready to have my say. And I'm learning. . .You can take it. You don't get mad at me. You don't punch back. You simply let me have my tantrum and then draw me into Your arms to whisper sweet truths that bring healing and clarity. Thank You for giving me the opportunity to "wrestle out" my faith, Lord. Amen.

Day 72

OUR REFUGE

The LORD Almighty is the one you are to regard as holy. . . . He will be a holy place.

ISAIAH 8:13–14 NIV

When you live in awe of God—when He alone is Lord of your life—you have nothing to fear. If fears or enemies assail you, a place of refuge is always nearby. God never throws His children to the wolves. Instead, He protects them in His holy place. With Jesus as your Savior, you always have a peaceful place of shelter.

PRAYER

As a kid I always had my favorite hiding places. Only, I could never hide from You, could I, Lord? My little cubby under the stairs. My closet. The attic. I loved exploring quiet set-apart places where I could be alone to think and pray. Now I see that You were my hiding place all along. I don't have to look for a physical spot; I have You! I can run into Your arms when I have questions or when I'm hurting. You're my refuge, my shelter. Thank You for that reminder today, heavenly Father! Amen.

Day 73

GIRLFRIENDS

And our hope for you is firm, because we know that just as you share in our sufferings, so also you share in our comfort.

2 CORINTHIANS 1:7 NIV

Anne of Green Gables was right: Bosom friends are important. Girls need girlfriends—little girls and grown-up girls alike. God wired us to need each other, to yearn for the heart-bonding that results from sharing sufferings, comfort, hugs, and giggles. Nothing's wrong with men, of course, but they don't make the same bosom friends as girls. Have you thanked the Lord lately for your soul sisters?

PRAYER

Lord, today I want to pause to thank You for my friends. You've placed amazing women in my life, and I'm so grateful for them. I'm ever thankful for the older ones, who mentor and guide me. And I also treasure the younger ones, the ones looking up to me for advice. More than anything, I'm happy to have the companionship of other female believers in my life. What an encouragement they are to me! They share my hardships and my joys. In so many ways they're just like family! Thank You for these special gals! Amen.

Day 74

RECEIVE HIS STRENGTH

The L*ORD* *also will be a refuge for the oppressed, a refuge in times of trouble.*

PSALM 9:9 NKJV

The psalms often speak of God as a refuge. Whether you're facing a trial of massive proportions (like oppression) or something much smaller, He wants you to turn to Him for help. Size doesn't matter, but your trust in Jesus does. Nothing you face is a shock to Him—He knows your troubles and has not deserted you. So go to your refuge and take strength from Him.

PRAYER

I've been in a lot of storms, Lord, and I know what it's like to take shelter. I usually head for the safest room in the house, the one with no windows. Once inside, I stay there until the winds die down. In so many ways, You are like that safe room. You're the place I know to go to when the winds start to howl. Any other place—or person—will leave me vulnerable. I need my rock. My shelter. My refuge. Thank You for always being there for me in my times of trouble, Lord. You've never left me alone, and I'm so grateful. Amen.

Day 75

HEAVEN'S BAKERY

"Those who hope in me will not be disappointed."

ISAIAH 49:23 NIV

As I stood in line ogling luscious pastries in the coffee shop's glass case, I asked the teenage clerk which she would suggest. Casting cornflower-blue eyes heavenward, she tapped her dainty chin with one finger before answering in a wistful voice, "I recommend the blueberry cheesecake. When I eat it, I hear angels." What higher recommendation is there? What greater hope have we than heaven? (Maybe we'll even enjoy blueberry cheesecake there!)

PRAYER

I love to think about heaven, Lord. I can only imagine what it's going to be like. A thousand times better than earth. No, a million! Streets of gold. Mansions. Gates of pearl. It's going to be remarkable. I try to keep heaven's joys in mind when I'm struggling here on earth. When my bank account is low. When I'm overworked and haven't had enough sleep. When I can't seem to keep up with all of the busyness. I think to myself, "One day. . .one day heaven will be mine." And that puts everything into perspective! I can't wait. Amen.

Day 76

A STORY OF FAITH

Looking unto Jesus the author and finisher of our faith.
HEBREWS 12:2 KJV

God is writing a story of faith through your life. What will it describe? Will it be a chronicle of challenges overcome, like the Old Testament story of Joseph? Or a near tragedy turned to joy, like that of the prodigal son? Whatever your account says, if you love Jesus, the end is never in question. Those who love Him finish in heaven, despite their trials on earth. The long, weary path ends in His arms. Today, write a chapter in your faithful narrative of God's love.

PRAYER

It's fun to think of You as the author of my life, Lord. You know all of the pages, even the ones that aren't written yet. That gives me great confidence! You're an amazing storyteller, so I know I can trust You with whatever's coming next. You're also the "finisher" of my faith. That means You know my story all the way to the very end. You plan to take me all the way. No stone will be left unturned as You carry me to the finish line. I can't wait to see what You have ahead for me. It's going to be amazing! Amen.

Day 77

BEYOND THE HORIZON

Always continue to fear the Lord. You will be rewarded for this; your hope will not be disappointed.

Proverbs 23:17–18 NLT

Have you ever traversed a long, winding road, unable to see your final destination? Perhaps you were surprised by twists and turns along the way or jarred by unexpected potholes. But you were confident that if you stayed on that road, you would eventually reach your destination. Likewise, God has mapped out our futures. The end of the road may disappear beyond the horizon, but we are assured that our destination will not be disappointing.

PRAYER

I'm always wishing I could see into the future, Lord. It's not that I don't trust You—though sometimes it's hard. It's just that I want to have a heads-up before something happens. I like to be prepared. You keep me guessing, though! With You, life is always an adventure. But I'm not afraid. I do trust You. I know You have my path all laid out, and I will walk it with Your hand in mine. I can't see it all yet, but I don't need to. Knowing that You'll be traveling with me, leading the way, is really all I need. Amen.

Day 78

SPIRITUAL CERTAINTY

We live by faith, not by sight.
2 CORINTHIANS 5:7 NIV

There is more than one way of seeing. We view the world around us with our eyes, but by doing so, we don't apprehend all there is in life. Those things we "see" by faith can't be perceived by our physical eyes. That's why doubters disbelieve them. But when God speaks to our hearts, it's as real as if we'd observed the truth plainly in front of us. Like Paul said, though our eyes cannot see it, we have a spiritual certainty.

PRAYER

Sometimes I feel I can see You everywhere, Lord—in a baby's smile, in an ocean wave, in a snowcapped mountain! Other times, I can't seem to locate You at all, no matter how far and wide the search. Through it all, I'm learning that You're always there, whether I see You or not. Thank You for the reminder that I won't always behold You with my physical eyes. I want to believe even when I can't see. I want to trust even when the situation in front of me makes no sense. May I always live by faith, not by sight, Lord! Amen.

Day 79

KINGDOM-PURPOSED FRIENDSHIP

"I tell you, use worldly wealth to gain friends for yourselves, so that when it is gone, you will be welcomed into eternal dwellings."

LUKE 16:9 NIV

There is a good way to use the things of the world, and Jesus describes it here. God gives us worldly wealth so we can share with others, making use of it to further God's kingdom. Though we may not have more than a pot of soup and some bread to offer, those things can be the start of a kingdom-purposed friendship. What do you have that God can use this way?

PRAYER

Lord, I want to use every single thing You give me to build and develop relationships for Your kingdom. There have been seasons when my offerings were meager. My pantry was short on supplies. But even then You somehow always used what I offered. I feel the same way about my talents and abilities. I have limits there too. But You can—and do—use every single thing to minister to those around me, and I'm loving being part of the process! I'm a very wealthy gal! Amen.

Day 80

WHO DO YOU FEAR?

"I tell you, my friends, do not be afraid of those who kill the body and after that can do no more."
LUKE 12:4 NIV

Who do you fear? If you fear anyone other than God, take heart. You need not concern yourself with anything that person can do to you. Even those who can take your life can't change your eternal destination. So if someone doesn't like your faith, don't sweat it. Put your trust in God and serve Him faithfully, and you need not fear.

PRAYER

I confess, Lord, I'm sometimes afraid of this big, scary world. I look around and see how crazy things have gotten and fear wells up inside of me. I'm grateful for the reminder that I have nothing to fear. The people—and circumstances—of this world can't affect me eternally. My future is secure in You, and only in You. So today I choose to focus on eternal things, not the noneternal. I want only the things that truly matter to consume my thoughts and propel me to action. Thanks for the reminder that I can be heavenly minded, Father! Amen.

Day 81

NEVER ALONE

I am convinced that nothing can ever separate us from God's love. Neither death nor life, neither angels nor demons, neither our fears for today nor our worries about tomorrow—not even the powers of hell can separate us from God's love.

ROMANS 8:38 NLT

I read a poll that said being alone is one of women's worst fears. When we experience loss, we sometimes feel that we're struggling all alone; that others around us can't possibly comprehend the scope of our fears, our worries, our pain. But the Bible says we're not alone, that nothing can separate us from our heavenly Father. He is right there beside us, loving us, offering His companionship when we have none.

PRAYER

Aloneness can seem overwhelming, Father. Sometimes, despite being physically surrounded by people, I still have that sense of being alone in this world. (I wonder, does everyone feel this way?) It's a good thing You've promised You'll never leave or forsake me. I often need that reminder in the alone times so that I don't sink into a pit of despair. With You at my side, I'm able to face any obstacles life throws in my path. I'm so grateful for Your companionship and Your love! Thank You, Lord! Amen.

Day 82

DISCONNECT FROM THE WORLD

Whosoever therefore will be a friend of the world is the enemy of God.
JAMES 4:4 KJV

There are good friendships and bad ones. When Christ becomes your best friend, other relationships may become distant. Old friendships based on secular interests no longer seem so attractive. Your lifestyles clash, and those friends become confused about the change in you. But this separation is part of God's plan of holiness. Jesus disconnects you from the world and draws you close to His people—Christian friends who share your love for Him. Together you may reach out to those old friends for Jesus too.

PRAYER

It's getting easier to draw the lines, Lord. I look at the friends I once spent time with, how they've chosen darkness over light, and I realize that staying connected is both unhealthy and dangerous. I'm so grateful for the godly friends You've placed in my path. They share my beliefs, my passions, and my joy for life. More than anything, they can be trusted to pour into my life—positive things that can change me for the better. May I be that kind of friend to others, I pray. And may I always stick close to You, my very best friend! Amen.

Day 83

PURE AND UNSPOILED

And everyone who has this hope set on Him purifies himself, just as He is pure.

1 JOHN 3:3 NASB

Don't you just love taking the first scoop of ice cream from a fresh half gallon? There's something about the smooth surface of unspoiled purity that satisfies the soul. It's the same with new jars of peanut butter, freshly fallen snow, or stretches of pristine, early morning beach sand. God looks at us that way—unblemished, unspoiled, and pure—because of our faith and hope in Him. Allow that thought to bring a smile to your face today.

PRAYER

Unspoiled. Pure. Oh, how I love those words, Lord! I think of them when I see a baby's innocent face or a puppy's wagging tail. This world is mostly impure, so when I encounter something as pure as a snowcapped mountain peak or a sandy white beach, my heart floods with joy. It's refreshing! When I read in Your Word that You can make all things new, I feel that same way. You can take my crusty old heart and make it as pure as that fresh-fallen snow. Thank You for renewing and refreshing me, Lord. Amen.

Day 84

GETTING WHAT YOU GIVE

Whoever sows sparingly will also reap sparingly,
and whoever sows generously will also reap generously.
2 CORINTHIANS 9:6 NIV

What you give is what you get. That's true in life, and it's also true spiritually. Anyone who tries to hold finances close will be letting go of spiritual blessings, while the person who shares generously gains in so many ways. It's hard to give up worldly treasures, but when you give in the name of Jesus, you will never run short.

PRAYER

I'll admit it, Lord—sometimes I cling too tightly to the things You've given me. Finances. Possessions. Talents. Abilities. I won't let anyone or anything pry them from my tightly clenched fist! But You want me to live with generosity leading the way. That means I have to open my hands and allow those things to be shared with the ones in my pathway. I will do my best to sow generously, Lord, not just so that I can reap generously but so that others can be blessed as well. Thank You for the reminder that my giving pleases Your heart. Amen.

Day 85

THE PALM OF HIS HAND

If I ride the wings of the morning, if I dwell by the farthest oceans, even there your hand will guide me, and your strength will support me.

PSALM 139:9–10 NLT

Surf foamed around my ankles as I lifted the burgundy starfish, its pointed tips curled in taut contraction. "It's okay, little fellow, I'll help you," I crooned, gently cradling the sea creature stranded by the outgoing tide. Tiny tentacles tickled my palm as the starfish relaxed, safe and protected. Likewise, God's hand rescues us, supports us, and guides us to life-sustaining waters when we're stranded. We're safe in the palm of His hand.

PRAYERS

There are days when I feel stranded, Lord, alone and abandoned. But then the warmth and comfort of Your hand sweeps in, lifting me and returning me to the life-giving environment I need to survive. Even on those days when I struggle to thrive, You remind me that I'm never outside the circle of Your care. You will protect me. You will sustain me. You will fight my battles for me. The palm of Your hand is the safest place I can possibly dwell, so today I choose to spend every moment with You. Thank You for Your protection, Lord! Amen.

Day 86

TURN TO HIM

"I will be a Father to you, and you shall be My sons and daughters, says the Lord *Almighty."*
2 CORINTHIANS 6:18 NKJV

Only unconfessed sin can separate you from the Father. But God never desires such distance. He wants to draw near, like a loving Father who holds His child, provides for her, and helps her at every turn.

Though your earthly father was or is less than perfect, your heavenly Father is not. He heals your hurts, helps you work through your problems, and offers His love at every turn. All you need to do is turn to Him in love.

PRAYER

Sometimes I get distressed thinking about how the people in this world have let me down. There have been plenty of disappointments and lots of pain. And some, in spite of their promises to never leave me, have long since gone their way. These letdowns have made me even more grateful to You, Lord! You will never break Your promise. You're perfectly good, perfectly kind, and perfectly devoted to me. No matter what I face, You're right beside me, loving me and reminding me that You're in this relationship—forever! Thank You, Lord! Amen.

Day 87

CHERISHED DESIRE

God our Father loves us. He treats us with undeserved grace and has given us eternal comfort and a wonderful hope.

2 THESSALONIANS 2:16 CEV

Webster's definition of hope: "to cherish a desire with anticipation." In other words, to hope is to yearn for something wonderful that you expect to occur. Our hope in Christ is not just a longing for something wonderful, as in "I hope for a sunny beach day." It's a deep trust with roots that extend from the beginning of time to the infinite future. Our hope is not just the anticipation of heaven but the expectation of a fulfilling life as we walk beside our Creator and best friend.

PRAYER

My hope is built on You, Lord, not the things of this world. I've tried—in times past—to put my hope in people, places, and things. It never worked out well. You, though? You've never let me down, not even once. So my yearning, my sense of expectation? It's placed solely in You, my Savior, the one who knows me best and loves me most. You've given me a wonderful sense of anticipation for what You're going to do in my life. I'm open to the possibilities because I know I can trust You. Thank You for being my hope giver, Lord! Amen.

Day 88

NOTHING IS HIDDEN

Nothing in all creation is hidden from God's sight.

HEBREWS 4:13 NIV

Good or bad, nothing escapes God's notice. Nothing is unknown to the Creator of the universe. And because He knows all, we can trust Him completely. He protects us from the wicked and supports the good in our lives because He knows just how both will affect us. When sorrow or trouble comes our way, we can count on His using it to benefit us—here and in eternity.

PRAYER

You have X-ray vision, Lord! You see it all—the good, the bad, and the ugly. And Your vision comes with a heightened sense of perception. You see and You understand. Me? I don't see much, other than what's right in front of me. And sometimes I get overwhelmed when what I see is negative. I can't yet envision how You're going to work these seemingly bad things for good in my life. Thank You for the reminder that You have created a bright future for me. Today I put my trust and confidence in You, the one who sees it all! Amen.

Day 89

FIRST LOVE

But you must stay deeply rooted and firm in your faith. You must not give up the hope you received when you heard the good news.
COLOSSIANS 1:23 CEV

Do you remember the day you turned your life over to Christ? Can you recall the flood of joy and hope that coursed through your veins? Ah, the wonder of first love. Like romantic love that deepens and broadens with passing years, our relationship with Jesus evolves into a river of faith that endures the test of time.

PRAYER

Ah, love! It's such a blissful, wonderful feeling! Love makes me want to put down roots, Lord, to stay grounded in the one responsible for those heart flutters! You are truly my first love. When I gave You my heart, I knew at once that it would be a forever thing. You offered me joy, peace, hope, and, best of all, eternal life! (Those are far better gifts than a dozen red roses, for sure!) And You're still proving Your love to me, day in and day out. Ours is a relationship that has lasted for years, Lord, and will go on into eternity. How I love You! Amen.

Day 90

HE IS FAITHFUL

Blessed are those whose help is the God of Jacob. . . . He remains faithful forever.

PSALM 146:5–6 NIV

You are not the only one who has experienced God's faithfulness. Through the years, countless believers have experienced His provision. Read Old Testament accounts of those who have never seen Him fail. Recall His acts in the New Testament as He showed the church that it could trust Him. God cannot fail His children, and He will not fail you. Trust in the God of Jacob, and pass on your testimony of His faithfulness.

PRAYER

The Bible—Your Word—is better than any movie I could ever watch! It's loaded with stories of Your intervention. You've been the hero of the story from day one, for sure! So when I begin to doubt Your goodness, I'll go back and watch the movie again. I'll remind myself how You saved the Israelites from the Egyptians. I'll feel myself emboldened as I watch those walls around Jericho fall. And best of all, I'll celebrate that the Savior of the world, the King of all kings, gave His life for me! Amen.

Day 91

ASTOUNDING RESCUE

Then I remember something that fills me with hope. The Lord's kindness never fails!

LAMENTATIONS 3:21–22 CEV

With our hectic lifestyles, pausing to remember the past isn't something we do very often. But perhaps we should. Then when doubts assault our faith, fears threaten to devour us, and disaster hovers like a dark cloud, we'll remember God's past loving-kindnesses. Hope will triumph over despair. Keeping a prayer journal is a wonderful way to chronicle answered prayer. We'll always remember the times when God's merciful hand rescued us in astounding ways.

PRAYER

I like to perform random acts of kindness whenever I can, Lord! And it's always fun when people are kind to me in surprising ways. Their little acts don't always stick with me for long, but when You shower me with kindness? I definitely remember those moments. You are truly a good, good Father. You pour out blessings on Your kids, even when we don't deserve them. These blessings serve as a reminder of how much You love us. And as a result, my soul is flooded with hope. Thanks for loving us so well. Amen.

Day 92

ALL-POWERFUL

God is our refuge and strength, an ever-present help in trouble.

PSALM 46:1 NIV

When we face serious troubles, people often cannot provide the solution. Limited by human frailty, even the most generous of them can only help us so much. In every trouble, we have a greater asset if we believe in Jesus. Our all-powerful Creator offers protection from harm and strength for the longest trial. He always wants to come to our aid. Facing a trouble of any size? Turn to Him today.

PRAYER

I like the idea that You're ever-present, Lord. I don't have to wait around for You to show up and save the day. I'm not staring at my watch and wondering if You're going to make an appearance. You're already there, in the thick of it (unlike some of the people who didn't come through in my life). You offer immediate protection, swift help, and enough courage to get me through all that I'm facing. Your presence brings peace, comfort, and an overall sense of well-being because I know I'm cared for by someone who adores me. Thank You, Lord! Amen.

Day 93

KEEPING US IN STITCHES

The secret things belong to the Lord our God.
DEUTERONOMY 29:29 NIV

Have you ever noticed the messy underside of a needlepoint picture? Ugly knots, loose threads, and clashing colors appear random, without pattern. Yet if you turn it over, an exquisite intricate design is revealed, each stitch blending to create a beautiful finished picture. Such is the fabric of our lives. The knots and loose threads may not make sense to us, but the Master Designer has a plan. The secret design belongs to Him.

PRAYER

Okay, I'll admit it: I'm a mess underneath it all, Lord. I do my best to hide it from a watching world, but if they look closely they'll see that I'm barely holding on at times. I'm a twisted mess of frayed knots and clashing colors, just like the backside of that needlepoint picture. Thank goodness You don't care. You remind me that the picture is still under construction. Best of all, You have this uncanny way of turning ugly into beautiful. You take my mess and turn it into something lovely. Thank You for that transformative power, Lord! Amen.

Day 94

NEVER FORGOTTEN

Who is like the Lord our God, . . .who stoops down to look on the heavens and the earth?

Psalm 113:5–6 NIV

This all-powerful Lord, to whom the heavens and earth are small, cares not just for the universe but for you. The verses that follow these describe His love for even the humblest person. Though you may face times of struggle, your awesome Lord will never forget you. One day, as verse 8 of this psalm promises, even the humble will sit with princes.

PRAYER

"She thinks she's all that." How often have I used that phrase, Lord? Some people really do think they're the cat's meow! They're puffed up, full of themselves. But when it comes right down to it, they're just human like the rest of us—flawed and incomplete. You, though? You're everything! You're the Creator of the universe, the one who flung the stars into space and who holds all things together. You are all-powerful, all-knowing, and all-sufficient. In short, You're all I need! Thank You for that reminder today, Lord! Amen.

Day 95

ONE HEFTY VERSE

To Him who is able to do far more abundantly beyond all that we ask or think, according to the power that works within us, to Him be the glory. . .forever and ever. Amen.

EPHESIANS 3:20–21 NASB

Don't you just love the bigness of this verse? It radiates with the enormity of God—the fact that nothing is beyond His scope or power. Read it aloud and savor the words "far more abundantly." Now repeat "beyond all that we ask or think" three times, pondering each word individually. Wow! If ever there was a hefty verse to cast an attitude of gratitude over our day, this is it. Yay, God!

PRAYER

Nothing is beyond Your scope or power, Lord! You're capable of going above and beyond what we could ask or think. It's remarkable, really, that Your powers are so vast! Then again, You did create the heavens and the earth, so I shouldn't be surprised that You're still working miracles today. The next time I begin to doubt Your ability to intervene in my situation, I'll remind myself that Your abilities exceed anything I can even begin to comprehend. Thank You, my great heavenly Father, for always being there for me! Amen.

Day 96

TENDER LOVE

This is love: not that we loved God, but that he loved us and sent his Son as an atoning sacrifice for our sins.

1 JOHN 4:10 NIV

We weren't sitting around thinking about loving God before He touched our lives. God began the process before we were even born. He sent His Son to bring us into communion with Him, and His Spirit drew us into a relationship with Him. We respond to God's overwhelmingly tender love when we invite Jesus into our lives. Even so, though many years of obedience can show our gratitude, they can never repay His loving compassion.

PRAYER

Sometimes I like to take credit for our relationship, Lord. I might say things like, "I found Jesus," or "I did this or that." The truth is, You found me. You loved me even before my mother conceived me in her womb. And You already had a plan for my life even then. So You get all of the credit, Lord! You're in charge, not me! And I'm learning to trust You more and more as my life story moves forward. Thank You for leading and guiding with such tenderness and love. I know I can trust You with all of my tomorrows because You've loved me through so many yesterdays. Amen.

Day 97

A LIFETIME AWARD

O Lord, you alone are my hope.
I've trusted you, O Lord, from childhood.
Psalm 71:5 NLT

My heart swelled like an overinflated balloon. Tears blurred my vision as little Josh bounded for the stage, his blond cowlick flopping in the breeze. As his second grade Sunday school teacher, I had worked tirelessly to help him memorize ten Bible verses. Josh beamed at the shiny medal encircling his neck, but I knew his true reward was God's Word implanted in his heart to guide him for the rest of his life.

PRAYER

There's no greater thrill than watching a child give his or her heart to You, Lord! And if I've played a role in that journey? Well, the satisfaction makes my heart swell! Thank You for placing little ones in my path whom I can minister to. And thank You for giving me a childlike heart, one that seeks You as a little one would do. My prayer for this generation is that all of the children would come to know You, that they would overcome the evils of this dark world by committing their hearts and lives to You, the Savior, Jesus Christ. Amen.

Day 98

APPRECIATION FOR MERCY

The Lord your God is a merciful God;
he will not abandon or destroy you.

DEUTERONOMY 4:31 NIV

Even when we fail God, He does not fail us. He knows our frailty and has mercy when we come to Him seeking forgiveness and wanting to change our ways. Mercy never holds grudges or seeks revenge; instead, it wants the best for forgiven sinners. So our merciful Lord calls us to make changes that show we appreciate what He has done for us. Is some appreciation called for in your life?

PRAYER

How many times have You shown me mercy, Lord? Hundreds? Thousands? If I really knew the number it would be staggering. I mess up repeatedly—multiple times a day—and yet You always love me through each mistake. You gently pick me up, turn me around, and settle my feet on the ground beneath me so I can keep going. You dry my tears, kissing them away, then give me a pat on the back and say, "We've got this." In short, You show mercy and grace every single time. I'm so grateful. How I appreciate You, my merciful God! Amen.

Day 99

PERMISSION TO MOURN

When I heard this, I sat down on the ground and cried. Then for several days, I mourned; I went without eating to show my sorrow, and I prayed.
NEHEMIAH 1:4 CEV

Bad news. When it arrives, what's your reaction? Do you scream? Fall apart? Run away? Nehemiah's response to bad news is a model for us. First, he vented his sorrow. It's okay to cry and mourn. Christians suffer pain like everyone else—only we know the source of inner healing. Disguising our struggle doesn't make us look more spiritual. . .just less real. As with Nehemiah, our next step is to turn to the only true source of help and comfort.

PRAYER

There are days when I just want to cry my eyes out, Lord. The sobs come from a deep place—unexpected and sorrowful. I empty myself of the pain as best I can, then dry my eyes and point myself to You, the one whose shoulders are big enough to carry it all. Thank You for allowing me to vent. Thank You for offering comfort when I'm in those low places. And most of all, thank You for providing healing balm when I need it most. Without You, Lord, I don't know where I would be. I'm so grateful for Your TLC. Amen.

Day 100

JOY IN OUR TROUBLES

Great is your love, reaching to the heavens;
your faithfulness reaches to the skies.
PSALM 57:10 NIV

Has God's mercy touched your life so deeply that you wanted to shout His praises to the skies? That's how the psalmist felt as he trusted in God despite his troubles. When we look to God in our troubles, our burdened hearts can still find joy. Though we are small and weak, He is most powerful. His strength will overcome our deepest problems if only we let it.

PRAYER

I love when those moments of release come, Lord. When I realize Your faithfulness has carried me through. In those very special moments, songs of praise rise up in my soul. I find my arms lifting to the skies and worship coming from my healed heart. How do You do it? How do You take my broken mess and turn it into something so beautiful, so blessed? I'll never understand how, but I definitely understand why. You love me. It's so obvious! You love me so much that You pour Yourself out for me time and time again. How I praise You! Amen.

Day 101

PEBBLES

"I will give you a new heart and put a new spirit within you; and I will remove the heart of stone from your flesh and give you a heart of flesh."

EZEKIEL 36:26 NASB

So many things can harden our hearts: overwhelming loss; shattered dreams; even scar tissue from broken hearts, disillusionment, and disappointment. To avoid pain, we simply turn off our feelings. Our hearts become petrified rock—heavy, cold, and rigid. But God can crack our hearts of stone from the inside out and replace that miserable pile of pebbles with soft, feeling hearts of flesh. The amazing result is a brand-new, hope-filled spirit.

PRAYER

Thank You for the reminder that my heart needs to stay soft and pliable, Lord! In this crazy world it's easier to harden up, to put up walls. Sometimes I think I'm protecting myself that way. But You come in and massage the hard places, making them as tender as can be. You turn my stony heart into a heart of flesh, one capable of loving—You, myself, and others. Thank You for the work You've done in my life, Father. Sometimes I'm amazed when I see how far we have come together. I'm so grateful. Amen.

Day 102

OVERFLOWING MERCY

Israel, put your hope in the Lord, for with the Lord is unfailing love and with him is full redemption.

Psalm 130:7 NIV

Why hope in God even in dire situations? Because every one of His people greatly needs His overflowing mercy. Our lives are frail, but He is not. Jesus brings the redemption we require. No matter what we face, Jesus walks with us. We need only trust faithfully that His salvation is on the way.

PRAYER

When is the answer coming, Lord? When will I see a victory? Sometimes I feel like You've hit the pause button and I'm waiting, waiting, waiting to see the solution to the problem. Still, I won't give up. I won't give in. I will keep my hope in You, my unfailing God. I might not see the victory today, but if it's coming tomorrow, I want to be found faithful in the interim. No matter how exhausted I am, no matter how weak, I will keep standing. I will keep believing. I will keep hoping. I will keep trusting. In short, I will stick with You. Amen.

Day 103

DO A LITTLE DANCE

Then Miriam. . .took a tambourine and led all the women as they played their tambourines and danced.

EXODUS 15:20 NLT

Can you imagine the enormous celebration that broke out among the children of Israel after God miraculously saved them from Pharaoh's army? Even dignified prophetess Miriam grabbed her tambourine and cut loose with her girlfriends. Despite adverse circumstances, she heard God's music and did His dance. Isn't that our goal today? To hear God's music above the world's cacophony and do His dance as we recognize everyday miracles in our lives?

PRAYER

There are moments when nothing short of a praise dance will do, Lord! Nothing can hold me back from the dance floor—I have to celebrate with every fiber of my being! When those instances come, I'm so happy for the freedom to worship You with my whole heart. I don't have to worry about what others think as I take to the floor. My dignity is a nonissue. I'm not worried about my ability as a dancer. I'm simply a girl overcome with love for her King, grateful for His input in her life. Thank You for freeing me up to dance, Father! Amen.

Day 104

TRUST GOD

Abraham answered, "God himself will provide the lamb for the burnt offering, my son."
GENESIS 22:8 NIV

Though God had commanded Abraham to sacrifice his son Isaac, the patriarch had faith that his son would not die. All it took was a ram caught in a bush. Because of Abraham's faith, the sheep was just where he needed it at the right moment. God provided just what was necessary—a sacrifice and a living son. Do you need God's provision today? Trust the God who made a way for Abraham to make a way for you too.

PRAYER

In the moment, it's not always easy to have faith. Sometimes fear grips my heart and I find myself looking, not for a ram in the bush but for a way out of the situation. Thank You for making provision even before I can see it, Lord. You're always faithful to provide what I need, even when my faith is weak. Build my trust, Lord! May I always have faith that the God who made a way for Isaac to live is, at this very moment, making sure I have everything I need too. Praise You, Father! Amen.

Day 105

PAYDAY

"Go into all the world and preach the gospel to all creation."
MARK 16:15 NASB

One day as our family discussed the Great Commission over dinner, my salesman husband asked my young daughter if she knew what *commission* meant. "Sure," she replied. "It's what you get paid at the end for what you did in the beginning."

Our commission will be paid in heaven when we're surrounded not only by dear friends and family with whom we shared our faith but by the souls reached by missions we supported with our time, money, and energies.

PRAYER

I love sharing Your love with those around me, Lord. It's one of the greatest honors of my life to share the message of Christ with a lost and dying world. And how wonderful it will be one day to stand in heaven next to those whose lives were touched by something I said or did. I'm also so grateful to the ones who poured into my life and led me to You. We'll throw a vast party in heaven, celebrating the victory of how we all came to know You because folks were not ashamed of the gospel message. May we always share Your good news with bravery! Amen.

Day 106

LET HIS LIGHT SHINE

For Christ's sake, I delight in weaknesses,
in insults, in hardships, in persecutions,
in difficulties. For when I am weak, then I am strong.
2 CORINTHIANS 12:10 NIV

Only God can make you strong in the weak places. In those spots of persecution and hardship, His power and grace shine through your fragile vessel as you live as a faithful Christian. When you feel broken and useless, trust in Him to fill your flaws, and His light will shine through the cracks of your pain and reach a hurting world.

PRAYER

Some days I just don't feel like shining, Lord. When I'm in a dark place, I feel there's nothing inside of me to give. I'm just too weak, too broken. Then You show up on the scene and remind me that even in the middle of my tribulation and pain, You can breathe life into me. You can take that situation and shed Your light on it. And once I become a reflection of You, there's plenty of light in me to share with others. Use my broken places to leak out the light of Your salvation, I pray. Amen.

Day 107

SOUL SISTER

"I always see the Lord near me, and I will not be afraid with him at my right side. Because of this, my heart will be glad, my words will be joyful, and I will live in hope."

ACTS 2:25–26 CEV

Laughter is the soul sister of joy; they often travel together. Humor is the primary catalyst for releasing joy into our souls and making our hearts glad. It's healthy for us too! Laughter is cleansing and healing, a powerful salve for the wounds of life, a natural medicine and tremendous stress reliever. Laughing is to joy what a "50 Percent Off" sign is to shopping. It motivates us to seek more, more, more!

PRAYER

No wonder Your Word says a merry heart is like good medicine, Lord. Laughter really does make me feel better, and not just psychologically. It's good for my body, my soul, and my spirit! Thank You for interrupting the not-so-great moments with hiccups of levity. They remind me that I don't have to be down in the dumps all the time, even when things aren't going my way. I can be transported—through joy—to a more hopeful place. I'm grateful for the gladness You've placed in my heart. Thanks for raining down joy in my life, Father! Amen.

Day 108

SAFE IN HIS WILL

Your hand will guide me, your right hand will hold me fast.
PSALM 139:10 NIV

Need to make a life-changing decision? God wants to be part of it. As the psalmist understood, allowing Him to guide your steps means you won't get off track and land in a nasty situation. For the believer, the best place to be is in the palm of God's hand, safe from harm and in the center of His will.

PRAYER

You're better than any GPS, Lord. You keep me on track, even when I'm tempted to veer off to the right or left. There are days when I don't know where to go and suddenly my feet begin to move, as if guided from on high. That's how I know You've got me covered! You take me places I never would have gone on my own. Thank You for walking alongside me and offering protection, Father. With my hand in Yours, I'm headed to some amazing places in the days ahead. Amen.

Day 109

JOY: JESUS OCCUPYING YOU

May all who fear you find in me a cause for joy, for I have put my hope in your word.

PSALM 119:74 NLT

Have you ever met someone you immediately knew was filled with joy? The kind of effervescent joy that bubbles up and overflows, covering everyone around her with warmth and love and acceptance. We love to be near people filled with Jesus-joy. And even more, as Christians, we want to be like them! Lord, remind us how.

PRAYER

Bubbling up, Lord! That's how I want to live. May joy radiate from my pores in such a way that the world can't help but notice. I'm not talking about the kind of fake joy so many seem to have. No, I want the real deal: Jesus-joy! And I know it can only come from a deep, abiding relationship with You. So fill me up to the top with Your joy and let it spill over onto all I come in contact with. May I be a contagious, effervescent vessel of hope, warmth, and love. Amen.

Day 110

EVERY STEP OF THE WAY

He will be our guide even to the end.
PSALM 48:14 NIV

When we're facing dire troubles, God never deserts us. As life ebbs away, He does not step back from our need. No, the eternal one guides us every step of the way, whether life is joyous or discouraging. God never gives up on you and never fails you. So don't give up on yourself. When times are hard, grab on to Him more firmly. He will never leave you or forsake you. And in the end, you will step into His arms in heaven.

PRAYER

I'm reminded of that old story about the footprints in the sand, Lord. There have truly been times in my life when You walked beside me and other times when You carried me. I suspect there have even been times when You had to drag me through the sand to get me to my destination point. No matter where life takes me, I will go with Your hand in mine. When I can't trust my own inner compass, I can definitely trust You. You've never failed me or led me astray, so I'll stick with You, Lord. Amen.

Day 111

AS THE TIDE TURNS

"He will not falter or be discouraged till he establishes justice on earth. In his teaching the islands will put their hope."

ISAIAH 42:4 NIV

Change. Besides our unalterable Lord, it's the only constant in this world. Yet the only person who likes change is a baby with a wet diaper. Isaiah prophesied that the Almighty will one day create positive change on earth. Like the tides that clean beach debris after a storm, positive change washes away the old and refreshes with the new. In the Lord's perfect plans we put our hope.

PRAYER

It feels like everything is speeding up now, Lord. The world seems to be moving at a faster pace, and I can hardly keep up. I'm trying to adapt to all of the changes, but some of them are leaving me dizzy. Discombobulated. I'm so grateful that the changes You have in mind are for my good, not my detriment. I'm learning to trust You with all of the twists and turns, even when they don't make sense. I know that in Your own time and Your own way, You will work all things together for my good and Your glory. So my hope remains in You! Amen.

Day 112

YOU CAN'T GO WRONG

"In your unfailing love you will lead the people you have redeemed. In your strength you will guide them to your holy dwelling."

EXODUS 15:13 NIV

By following Jesus, you always head in the right direction. Though the way may seem dark or convoluted and you might wonder if you're on the right track, as His Spirit leads you, you can't go wrong. Your powerful Lord directs you in His everlasting way. If you start to veer off track, He will guide your steps. God's love never deserts His obedient child.

PRAYER

All my life I've heard the expression "two steps forward, one step back," Lord. It seems that's how it often goes. I think I'm making progress, moving in the right direction, and then something happens to cause me to freeze up, to stop in my tracks. I have to backtrack a bit, then start over. I'm grateful for Your guidance, and not just during times like these. If it weren't for Your Spirit, I don't know where I would be. (Lost in a field, likely!) You're leading me and guiding every step. I'm truly grateful, Lord! Amen.

Day 113

UP IS THE ONLY OUT

Let them lie face down in the dust,
for there may be hope at last.
LAMENTATIONS 3:29 NLT

The Old Testament custom for grieving people was to lie prostrate and cover themselves with ashes. Perhaps the thought was that when you're wallowing in the dust, at least you can't descend any further. There's an element of hope in knowing there's only one way to go: up. If a recent loss has you sprawled in the dust, know that God doesn't waste pain in our lives. He will use it for some redeeming purpose.

PRAYER

I've been there, Lord! (Way too many times to count.) I've been face down in the dust, ready to give up. Thank goodness You've met me there time and time again. You picked me up, brushed me off, gave me a hug, and sent me on my way again. Sometimes I just need the reassurance that it's possible to keep going when I don't feel like it. (And I'll be honest, there are a lot of times I simply don't feel like it.) I'm grateful for the reminder that You meet me in my pain and You care. You won't let one moment of it go to waste. Thank You, Father! Amen.

Day 114

UNFAILING LOVE

The Lord delights in those who. . .
put their hope in his unfailing love.
Psalm 147:11 NIV

We can hope in a lot of things that fail us miserably, or we can enjoy a blind optimism that leads us into trouble. But when we hope in God, who has loved us completely, our faith cannot fail. Could the one who delights in our trust forget to bless our anticipation of an eternity with Him?

Make God joyful today as you put your trust in His everlasting love.

PRAYER

I don't want to be found guilty of putting my trust in anything or anyone besides You, Lord. Oh, I've done it in the past. I trusted in my job. My employer. The government. My friends. My family. None of those things are bad, but You want me to learn to place my full trust in You, so I'm choosing to do that today. I know I make Your heart glad when I shift my focus from things—and people—back to You. You're the giver of all, so I need to remind myself that You are also my supplier. Today I put my hope and my trust in You. You've never let me down! Amen.

Day 115

WELCOME BACK

Train up a child in the way he should go:
and when he is old, he will not depart from it.
PROVERBS 22:6 KJV

I'll never forget the tender bedtime family gatherings on my sister's bed when I was a child. After reading a Bible story from the big picture Bible, we took turns praying. When I had children, I established the same tradition in our home. The Bible promises that if we instill God's Word and principles in our children, they will one day return to that foundation. It may take time, but God's Word will not return void.

PRAYER

How precious is the faith of a child, Lord! I remember the tender way You wooed me when I was young. I loved family prayers. I enjoyed Sunday school. And even now that I'm a grown woman I still have the faith of that little girl. I look to You as my Daddy-God, the one I run to when I need comfort or guidance. May we always train up the little ones to love You from an early age so that they will never depart from You as they grow older. I take Proverbs 22:6 as both a mandate and a blessing. Let the little ones come to You! Amen.

Day 116

PROSPERITY RETURNS

"Then I will compensate you for the years that the swarming locust has eaten."

JOEL 2:25 NASB

Those of us who rejoice in God can trust that even though the consuming locusts of life may destroy our blessings, God will replace them. Though hardship may cause us to struggle awhile, God will turn the situation around and pour out blessings on His faithful people. Prosperity returns to those who love Him well. In heaven or on earth, the blessing appears again.

PRAYER

There have been some deep losses in my life, Lord. Many made no sense at all. I blamed You. . .I blamed others. . .I even blamed myself. And if I'm being brutally honest, I wanted to give up. Then You swept in and turned those situations around. You made provision. You filled in the gap, bringing joy where once there had been sorrow. You gave back after the enemy stole from me. Now that I see how You operate, I know I can trust You—with all of my tomorrows. You will make sure I have everything I need. How grateful I am! Amen.

Day 117

SEASONS OF BLESSING

There shall be showers of blessing.
EZEKIEL 34:26 KJV

Don't you enjoy walking through seasons of extraordinary blessing? We can hardly believe it when God's "more than enough" provision rains down upon us. What did we do to deserve it? Nothing! During such seasons, we can't forget to thank Him for the many ways He is moving in our lives. Our hearts must overflow with gratitude to our gracious and almighty God.

PRAYER

Father God, thank You. I am so grateful for the many blessings You have showered on me. When I think back on my life, I realize I have enjoyed many seasons of Your extraordinary favor. And although I have done my best to follow You, I am only human—and I have failed time and time again. Yet You still choose me. . .You still love me. . .You still give me Your best. On my own I could never be "good enough" to deserve all You've done for me. But because of Your goodness and grace, You accept me as I am—imperfections and all. Every day You gift me, Father, I will choose to follow You. I love You!

Day 118

PRAISE GOD—NO MATTER WHAT

The king will rejoice in God;
all who swear by God will glory in him.
PSALM 63:11 NIV

Need some joy in your life? Start praising God, and no matter what messy situations you face today, you'll begin rejoicing. Praise Him for who He is—for His immense, loving nature that has blessed you so much. Thank Him for the love He has showered on you. As you remember His love, sorrow will lose its grip on your life.

PRAYER

Thank You for the promise that I can praise my way through, Lord! I'm reminded of the story in the Old Testament about Jehoshaphat, who faced a formidable foe. He put his worshippers at the front of the battle lines, and they led the way with praise. That's what I need to do, even when I don't feel like it. (*Especially* when I don't feel like it!) When I lead with praise, the battles are won. Things might get a little messy on the way to the battlefield, but joy will come as the battles are won. Thank You for that reminder! Amen.

Day 119

ROCKY ROAD

Through the Spirit we eagerly await by faith the righteousness for which we hope.

GALATIANS 5:5 NIV

My daughter's five-pound Russian terror (oops—that's terrier) is anything but righteous. Rocky dashes after cars, nibbles poisonous plants, and routinely ingests ripped-apart rugs. In order to guide said pup along the path of righteousness, doors must close. In a similar way, our paths of righteousness are guided by one who shuts doors according to what's best for us. So, girlfriends—enough howling, whining, and scratching at closed doors!

PRAYER

I get it, Lord. You often close doors. . .on purpose. You do so for our safety. Our paths of righteousness are carefully guarded by You, the only one who knows what's coming next in our lives. You serve as protector and shield, whether we're on a rocky road or a straight and narrow path. You can see beyond the bends in the road and You have great plans for us. I will keep my trust in You, no matter how twisted the journey might become. Open doors that need to be opened, Lord, and slam shut the ones You want me to avoid. Amen.

Day 120

GOD IS GREAT

I know that the L*ORD is great, that our Lord is greater than all gods.*

PSALM 135:5 NIV

Other "gods" contend with Jesus in the marketplace of ideas, and devout Christians may encounter contention. But just as the psalmist recognized God's greatness, we can too as we look at the world around us. No other would-be deity shows forth its glory in creation. No other has provided God's gracious salvation. If Jesus is Lord of our lives, how can we look to any other gods?

PRAYER

All my life I've heard of big-G God and little-g gods. The little g's have nothing on You, Lord! There's only one true God in all of the universe. No matter how loudly the world shouts otherwise, You are the only one great enough to rule over it all. There are plenty of counterfeits out there, but none of them stand the test of time. Only You, Lord. You are in control of my life, and I submit myself to Your authority and Your will. Thank You for the reminder that You are our big-G God! Amen.

Day 121

NOT SUZIE HOMEMAKER

The Spirit has given each of us a special way of serving others.

1 CORINTHIANS 12:7 CEV

My friend Denise has the gift of hospitality. She welcomes people into her home and makes them feel loved through her thoughtful accents: serving food on her best china, lighting scented candles, offering cozy furnishings. Hospitality is not my gift. My guests get bagged chips and flat soda and leave coated in cat hair. God taught me not to compare and despair, for He has given each of us our own gift to be used for His service. What's yours?

PRAYER

I feel this, Lord. Deeply. I compare my own talent in hospitality to that of other women and I fall flat. My attempts seem feeble at best. Counterfeit, even. But You are showing me that a hospitable woman opens her heart to others in her own way. She's not a copycat, trying to be like others. She uses her unique giftings and abilities to draw in the people God has placed in her path. May I be that kind of friend to others, Lord, the kind who says, "The house is a mess, but who cares? C'mon in!" Amen.

Day 122

LIVE DEVOTEDLY

Do you not know that you are the temple of God and that the Spirit of God dwells in you?
1 CORINTHIANS 3:16 NKJV

God lives within you, not in a distant place. When you act according to His Word, He acts. But when you fail to act according to His Word, people may begin to doubt Him. That's why Paul encourages you to live devotedly for your Lord. As one of His people, you're filled with His potent Spirit, who empowers you to live a holy life. Live in His strength always.

PRAYER

I love to watch the devoted ones, Lord. They care for loved ones in pain. They tend to the needs of the elderly parent with Alzheimer's. They take meals to those in need. All around me, these devoted men and women are Your hands and feet, caring for others with as much grace as You would offer personally. May I be found just as grace-filled, just as holy! May I live a devoted life, caring for others the way You care for them. By the power of Your Spirit I want to make a difference in the lives of those I love. Amen.

Day 123

WORKING OUT

I will never give up hope or stop praising you.
PSALM 71:14 CEV

Praise is like a muscle: If we don't exercise it regularly, it becomes weak and atrophied. But if we flex an attitude of gratitude daily, praise grows into a strong, dependable force that nurtures hope and carries us through the worst of circumstances. Helen Keller, though blind and deaf, offered highest praise to her Creator: "I thank God for my handicaps, for through them, I have found myself, my work, and my God."*

PRAYER

I want to stay strong in my faith, Lord, and I know that praise plays a major role. Thank You for the reminder that praise really is like a muscle. I have to spend time in the spiritual gym to stay fit. There have been seasons when I've been complacent, Lord. Then, in Your gentle, sweet way, You remind me that I don't have to be weak. Through the power of praise I can be strong in You. So up I rise from the ashes, ready to begin my spiritual workout. I feel myself growing stronger by the moment as I put my hope in You and lift up Your name. How I praise You, Lord! Amen.

---

* Helen Keller, *The Story of My Life*, (Dover Publications, 1902)

Day 124

LOVE IS ACTION

Dear friends, let us love one another, for love comes from God. Everyone who loves has been born of God and knows God.

1 JOHN 4:7 NIV

Want to see love? Look at God. Seeking love in this world is bound to be confusing. But in our Lord, we see the clean, clear lines of real love—love we can share with our families, friends, and fellow believers. Love for our enemies. Love for our Savior. Apart from God, we cannot truly and sacrificially love others. Love isn't just a feeling—it's the actions we take as we follow our Lord.

PRAYER

It's not always easy to remember that love is more than a feeling, Lord. Sometimes, truth be told, I'm ruled by my feelings. I let them control me. But You're showing me a different type of love, the version that helps me care about not only friends and family but even my enemies. I can hardly comprehend this kind of love, but I long to share it. The only way I can is if I first accept Your love for me—a broken, wounded child. As I come to realize the height and depth of Your love, I'll be more and more eager and equipped to share it with others. Thank You for teaching me to love! Amen.

Day 125

INEXPLICABLE STRENGTH

"The joy of the LORD is your strength."
NEHEMIAH 8:10 NIV

Joy is not based on the circumstances around us. It is not synonymous with happiness. God promised believers His deep, abiding joy—not fleeting happiness, which is here today, gone tomorrow. The joy of the Lord rises above external situations and supernaturally overshadows everything else to become our inexplicable, internal strength.

PRAYER

How can I explain the unexplainable, Lord? This joy You've given me is beyond comprehension and completely indescribable. That's because it's otherworldly. It makes no sense to the natural mind to have a full heart even in the midst of tragedy and pain. Only through You is such a thing possible. I'm grateful for this true, authentic joy because it doesn't come and go depending on my circumstances. It abides deep within me, ready to spring forth just when I need it. Thanks for being a joy-giving God! Amen.

Day 126

SEEING GOD

No one has seen God at any time. If we love one another, God abides in us, and His love has been perfected in us.

1 JOHN 4:12 NKJV

How do we see God? Often, it's through other people. That's why it's important to have a compassionate Christian witness—people see you and think God is like you if you claim His name. In that way, many people have picked up erroneous concepts about the Savior. But many more have come to love Him through faithful testimonies. Today, you can love others and show them clearly what Jesus looks like.

PRAYER

I confess, I haven't always been a good witness, Lord. There are times when my reflection of You is skewed. I get angry. Upset. I react, forgetting that people are watching me. I'm sure there have been times when they've said things like, "And she calls herself a Christian?" (*sigh*) Thanks for the chance to start fresh, Jesus. I want to be a compassionate Christian witness while staying true to my convictions and never compromising my faith. May I always remember that love can lead the way, even in the hardest of circumstances. Amen.

Day 127

FOREVER JOY

We don't look at the troubles we can see now. . . .
For the things we see now will soon be gone,
but the things we cannot see will last forever.
2 CORINTHIANS 4:18 NLT

A painter's first brushstrokes look like random blobs—no discernible shape, substance, or clue as to what the completed painting will be. But in time, the skilled artist brings order to perceived chaos. Initial confusion is forgotten in joyful admiration of the finished masterpiece.

We often can't see past the blobs of trouble on our life canvases. We must trust that the artist has a masterpiece underway and that there will be great joy in its completion.

PRAYER

You see the whole picture, Lord. You're not just looking at the "paint blobs" of today, but You see my whole life, from beginning to eternity. And because You see the entire picture, I can trust You to paint me as a masterpiece! (You don't make mistakes. Every stroke is a thing of beauty!) A day is coming when the chaos of today will be behind me and I'll see it as part of the whole. For now, thank You for the reminder that You work all things together for my good and for Your glory. This painting is going to be magnificent, Jesus! Amen.

Day 128

LIFE-ALTERING IMPACT

We were therefore buried with him through baptism into death in order that, just as Christ was raised from the dead through the glory of the Father, we too may live a new life.

ROMANS 6:4 NIV

Baptism is a picture of the death of the old, sinful nature and the new faith-life God gives those who trust in Him. Belief in Jesus has a life-altering impact. One moment a sinful person is dead, held in sin's grasp. The next she becomes an entirely new person, alive in her Savior. Only Jesus offers this glorious freedom. Has He given it to you?

PRAYER

"All things new." How I love those words, Lord! There's a lot of the old me that I'd like to forget. Mistakes were made. Complications arose. But You say that yesterday is behind me now and I need to focus on today, so that's what I'll do. Everything today is fresh and new, a story yet to be written. It's not tainted by my backstory (thank goodness). I'm grateful for fresh starts and happy to be looking ahead and not backward. Thank You for the reminder that all things truly can be made new in You! Amen.

Day 129

PERFECT LOVE

Love never gives up, never loses faith, is always hopeful, and endures through every circumstance.
1 CORINTHIANS 13:7 NLT

We have relationships in three directions: upward (with God), outward (with others), and inward (with ourselves). We are bound to be disappointed at one time or another by the latter two. Because of human frailty, we will inevitably experience failure by others and even ourselves. Our imperfect love will be strained to the breaking point. But our Creator will never fail us—His perfect love never gives up on us.

PRAYER

There's a reason I say You're my best friend, Lord. You never let me down. You never disappoint. I've had sad breakups and there have been people who've walked away from me at my lowest point. Their actions stung. They were like a knife to the heart. But You? You never walk away from me! So it's important that I maintain this, my most important relationship, because it sustains my very life. Thank You for never giving up on me and for enduring in love through all of the ups and downs. Amen.

Day 130

LIVING IN THE LIGHT

In him was life, and that life was the light of all mankind.
JOHN 1:4 NIV

Jesus is a Christian's life and light, as anyone who has walked with Him for a while can tell you. Everything is different once He enters a person's life. As a result, the new believer begins to make changes, cleaning out the dark corners of her existence so that the bright light shining within her won't fall on dirty places. She's living in the light, following Jesus.

PRAYER

I've never cared much for the dark, Lord. I stumble around, bumping into furniture and stubbing my toes. In preparation for the storms that come my way, I always keep flashlights and headlamps handy because I know I'm likely to get hurt without them. You are the best light of all. Your radiance is effective against the darkness of this world and the chaos of this current age. When I shine Your light on my circumstances, it gives me a clear sense of direction. Thank You for the reminder that I'm called to be a light for others, and thanks for always guiding me with Your light. Amen.

Day 131

THREE LITTLE WORDS

Three things will last forever—faith, hope, and love.
1 CORINTHIANS 13:13 NLT

Don't you get tired of throwing away holey socks? It's hard to believe that modern technology can scan quivers inside our livers and detect nickel-sized puddles on Mars, but we still can't manufacture socks that last. Yep, there are precious few things that endure: faith, hope, and love. Three things that will never break down, wear out, or get lost. These are the only things worth keeping.

PRAYER

"And now these three remain: faith, hope and love" (1 Corinthians 13:13 NIV). They survive the test of time, Lord. They roll right over from this life into eternity. How grateful I am! "But the greatest of these is love." I remember this verse from childhood, how it shaped my relationship with others and with You. It has propelled me to look at love as the key gift I can give others. I'm grateful for my faith in You and for the hope You've placed in my heart. And I'm especially thrilled that love is the greatest of all. I can't go wrong as long as I lead with love. Amen.

Day 132

YOU ARE VALUABLE

Who can find a virtuous woman?
for her price is far above rubies.
PROVERBS 31:10 KJV

Are you a virtuous woman? If so, you are truly valuable, no matter how unbelievers may criticize you. Proverbs 31 says you can have a profitable life characterized by good relationships, a happy home environment, and successful business ventures if you run your life according to God's principles. So don't worry about the opinions of others if they don't mesh with God's. Instead, obey Him and be a valuable jewel to your Lord.

PRAYER

Sometimes I read the word *virtuous* and want to run in the opposite direction, Lord. I feel unworthy. I wonder if I'll ever be like the Proverbs 31 woman. Then I'm reminded that it's Your virtue, not mine, that needs to shine through. I need to lean on You to be more like You. So as I set up house, as I live in relationship with family, friends, coworkers, and church members, may my focus always be on You. . .and not me. I'll fail every time. But You? Your virtue can come shining through as long as I always point others to You. Amen.

Day 133

NEW LIFE

God is so good, and by raising Jesus from death,
he has given us new life and a hope that lives on.
1 PETER 1:3 CEV

The words of a song I wrote while pregnant with my first child exult in the similarities between new physical life and fresh spiritual life in Christ: "New life stirs within me now. Like a soft breeze, transforming me now. It's a miracle of love, precious blessing from above. My heart has taken wings. . .lift me up!"

New life. By the goodness of God, we can experience this precious transformation that is no less miraculous than a baby growing within us.

PRAYER

Oh, how grateful I am for new life in You, Jesus! You've taken this broken shell of a human being and transformed her by Your love! You breathed fresh life into me, even when I didn't deserve it, and reworked my heart, making all things new. I love Your transformative power! The new me—energized by Your Spirit—rises above life's circumstances and cries out songs of praise, grateful for all You've done. That's the power of a life made new. (Have I mentioned how grateful I am?) Amen!

Day 134

LOVE AND OBEY

"Whoever has my commands and keeps them is the one who loves me."

JOHN 14:21 NIV

Do you feel you love God with all your heart? Then show it by obeying Him. Jesus paved the path for you. Through His own sacrificial life, He demonstrated what it means to obey the Father. A Christian who lives for herself rather than for God shows wavering commitment. One who loves God wholeheartedly walks in Jesus' way, obeying His commands in scripture. Here is where we start: Love God? Then obey Him too.

PRAYER

I'm not always the most obedient child, Lord. (This You already know.) There are times when I want to go my own way, listen to my own voice. But Your Word says that obedience is key to proving my love to You. If I love You, I'll obey Your commands. And I need to do so wholeheartedly, with joy leading the way. It's a sacrifice at times, sure, but I'm up for it! I want to prove my love for You with everything I do and every word I speak. Thanks for the reminder that walking in obedience is truly an act of love for You, my heavenly Father. Amen.

Day 135

TIME-OUT

"The Lord will not abandon His people."
1 Samuel 12:22 NASB

Do you remember when, as a little girl, you languished alone in your room as punishment? Or maybe you sat with your nose plastered to the corner in time-out. It felt like your parents had abandoned you, didn't it? As adults, we sometimes feel abandoned when that's not the case at all. We're actually in a place strategically chosen by a loving Father to teach us, broaden us, and improve us in the end.

PRAYER

You've put me in time-out a time or two, haven't You, Lord? I felt like a disciplined child, nose to the wall, pondering what led me to that state. But You never left me there, and I'm learning that You only discipline out of great love for me. You've never abandoned me or left me to my own devices (thank goodness!). I'm on a learning curve, but the key thing I've learned is that You will never leave me or forsake me. You're always right there, guiding, directing, and loving me through every bump in the road. I'm so grateful. Amen.

Day 136

BLESSINGS WILL COME

"All these blessings shall come upon you and overtake you, because you obey the voice of the Lord your God."
Deuteronomy 28:2 NKJV

Obey God; receive blessings. It seems simple enough, doesn't it? Then why do we obey and end up facing more trouble than before? Perhaps it's because we're looking at our circumstances from our perspective, not His. Blessings don't always follow on the heels of obedience; often they take time to appear. Today's blessings may result from long-ago faithfulness. But because God has promised, we know good things will come if only we wait.

PRAYER

I know my life isn't always going to be sunshine and rainbows, Lord. There will be hard times too. But how could I possibly overlook the daily blessings You pour out on me? I see those blessings in the eyes of my children. I witness them when I open my pantry door and find food inside. I see them again when friends and loved ones swoop in around me. They're obvious when I see money in my checking account. I'm truly blessed by You. So why wouldn't I obey a God who pours out His love and blessings on me? You make it easy, Lord! Amen.

Day 137

BIGGER AND BETTER

Waiting does not diminish us, any more than waiting diminishes a pregnant mother. . . . The longer we wait, . . .the more joyful our expectancy.

ROMANS 8:24–25 MSG

Life is filled with waiting—on slow people, transportation, doctor reports, even on God to act. Waiting often requires patience we don't have. It feels like perpetual pregnancy—anticipating a baby that is never delivered. The secret is to clasp hands with our Lord. He offers His shield of protection from impatience, irritability, and anger, replacing those things with self-control, kindness, and joy.

Waiting is inevitable, but we can draw closer to the Father in the waiting.

PRAYER

I haven't always done the best job of waiting, Lord. In fact, there have been times I've been downright impatient! But the blessings on the other side of waiting? Well, those make it all worthwhile! You're always "birthing" new things, if only I'll wait for them. So instead of complaining, I'll look forward, with anticipation, to the blessing that is to come. You're going to deliver something wonderful, and if I have to wait awhile to see it. . .well, that's what I'll do. Because I know I can trust You, Lord. Amen.

Day 138

INTO ETERNITY

*Blessed are they that do his commandments,
that they may have right to the tree of life,
and may enter in through the gates into the city.*
REVELATION 22:14 KJV

The blessings of obedience not only impact us today but follow us into eternity. Whatever we do to please God never dies. As we trust in Jesus, the works that demonstrate our faith give us joy now and remain secure for the future in the one who never changes. We look forward to life in the New Jerusalem even as we reap His blessings now.

PRAYER

It's kind of overwhelming to realize my actions have eternal consequences, Lord. What I do today can impact eternity. If I obey You and witness to others, one day I might see them in heaven. (What an awesome realization!) I can only imagine what heaven will be like, but it thrills my soul to know that I could impact the lives of others and lead them to a relationship with You. What fun heaven will be, filled with people whose lives were touched by my obedience here on earth. I can hardly wait! Amen.

Day 139

PLEASE RESCUE ME

I long for you to rescue me! Your word is my only hope.
PSALM 119:81 CEV

Have you ever longed to be rescued?

Stranded after shredding some knee ligaments during a remote mountain-skiing accident, I waited helplessly for rescuers to arrive. All alone on the raw Canadian mountainside, I felt fear mount. Freezing temperatures, prowling cougars, and unrelenting pain threatened to engulf me in despair. So I did the most and the least I could do: I prayed and recited scripture. And my faithful heavenly Father rescued me with His peace.

PRAYER

How many times have I needed rescue, Lord? A hundred? A thousand? Every time I found myself in a pit of despair, You swept in and performed a miracle. In other words, I lived to tell about it. Okay, some of those were eleventh-hour rescues. I wondered if You would come through, but then—like a flash of light—there You were! Thank You for those miraculous rescues! You are a God who cares about His children. You won't leave us stranded, even when the pit is one of our own digging. You truly love and care for Your own. How grateful I am! Amen.

Day 140

GOD HEARS

"Therefore I tell you, whatever you ask for in prayer, believe that you have received it, and it will be yours."

MARK 11:24 NIV

This verse is not prescribing some magical incantation but rather encouraging faith that God hears and answers our requests. When we trust that He knows our needs and wants to respond to them, we are in a position to receive.

Would Jesus be proud of our requests? Do we seek the good of others? Or do we look only to our own desires? God answers prayers that reflect His will. How do yours stack up against this measure?

PRAYER

Sometimes I feel like I'm talking to a brick wall when I call out to my spouse, kids, friends, or coworkers, Lord. They tune me out. Oh, I'm guilty of it too. We hear what we want to hear, I guess. But You? You hear it all. Even my weakest cries from the depths of my soul, You hear. And best of all, You come rushing in as if I'd shouted into a microphone! So today I won't hesitate to take my concerns to You. I know You'll listen and respond because You love me. How grateful I am for Your attentive care! Amen.

Day 141

HOPE RESURRECTED

We had hoped that he would be the one to set Israel free! But it has already been three days since all this happened.
LUKE 24:21 CEV

The scenario for this scripture is quite unusual. Two of Jesus' disciples are describing their lost hope due to the events surrounding Jesus' death to none other than Jesus Himself. They don't recognize Him as they walk together on the road to Emmaus after His resurrection. Spiritual cataracts blind them to the hope of their salvation—the Living Hope who is right in front of them! Let's open our spiritual eyes to Jesus, who is walking beside us.

PRAYER

I give up so easily, Lord! Sometimes I'm just like those disciples, counting down the days and saying, "Why hasn't He come through for me yet?" Only, of course, You already have! Your Word says the battles in my life are already won. I just have to walk them out. I have to remove my spiritual blinders to see the truth that You won't let me down. Today I choose to do just that. I'll keep hope alive as I put one foot in front of the other, and I won't give up no matter how tempting it might be! Amen.

Day 142

LOVE YOUR ENEMIES

"But I tell you, love your enemies and pray for those who persecute you."

MATTHEW 5:44 NIV

Without God's strength, could any of us follow this command of Jesus for more than a very brief time? Consistently loving an enemy is a real challenge. If you hurt from pain inflicted by another, you hardly want to pray for her. But loving actions and prayer can bring great peace between two people at odds with each other. For those who consistently follow this command, strife may not last forever.

PRAYER

It's hard, Lord! I'll admit it—this is an area I struggle in. I don't want to love my enemies. To turn the other cheek feels impossible much of the time, especially when someone has hurt me deliberately. But You say I need to love and pray for those who persecute me, so I'm willing to do it Your way. I receive Your peace when I offer forgiveness. Plus there's potential for reconciliation. So today I let go of my angst and release the people who've hurt me to You, and I pray for their hearts and their well-being as I do. Amen.

Day 143

SPRUNG

I will free your prisoners from death in a waterless dungeon. Come back to the place of safety, all you prisoners who still have hope!

ZECHARIAH 9:11–12 NLT

In the marvelous book *The Count of Monte Cristo*, Edmond Dantes is unjustly imprisoned. Against all odds, God enables him to escape and eventually return victorious, a hope-filled man.

Have you ever felt trapped in a prison of hopelessness? Financial difficulties, poor health, unemployment, a rocky marriage, delinquent children—there are countless dungeons that shackle us. But God promises hope and freedom from our prisons. Jesus bailed us out!

PRAYER

I've felt trapped so many times, Lord. By my circumstances. By financial despair. By broken relationships. By hopelessness. Life in the pit is no way to live. I'm not a fan of that "shackled" feeling, for sure. That's why I'm so glad You've promised to set me free—not just from many of the external things that bind me but from internal fears and worries as well. You stand by, ready to bust me out of every prison cell. So today I give a shout of praise and wait for the chains to break. You have better things for me to do than remain tethered to my problems. Amen.

Day 144

HEALING POWER

The prayer of faith will save the sick, and the Lord will raise him up. And if he has committed sins, he will be forgiven.

JAMES 5:15 NKJV

Have you seen the amazing healing power of prayer? As faithful Christians lift up a sufferer to God, He works not only in the body but also in the heart and soul. Know someone who is ill? Pray for physical health to return. But don't forget to include spiritual needs, for the Great Physician treats the whole person. Some spiritual issue may be the real problem that requires healing.

PRAYER

You are the great healer, Lord! And I'm so glad You don't limit Yourself to healing only physical suffering. There have been times my heart and mind were in worse shape than my physical body. You're interested in the whole of me—internal and external, natural and spiritual. So I give every part of myself to You today and ask for healing in all areas, even those I haven't acknowledged. Do a deep work, Father, as only You can. I submit myself to You like a patient to a doctor, knowing I'm in the best hands ever! Amen.

Day 145

POWER SOURCE

He gives strength to the weary and
increases the power of the weak.
ISAIAH 40:29 NIV

Sometimes we feel as if our backs will break under the burdens we carry: debt, responsibilities, impossible schedules. But our God promises to strengthen and empower us if we turn to Him for help. He knows. He cares. He is able.

It's been written that persecuted European Christians don't pray for God to lessen their loads like American Christians do. Instead, they pray for stronger backs.

PRAYER

I definitely need a stronger back, Lord! I feel like I'm carrying a lot. Oh, some of it is my own doing. I take on too much. But the rest of it? Ugh! It piles up like an overloaded backpack on the first day of school. I want to dump those books all over the ground and forget about them! But You know how to unburden me in a way that's beneficial to my overall well-being. So have Your way. Remove the things that need to be removed and show me how to walk with every area of my life in balance. Amen.

Day 146

PRAYER FROM THE HEART

Some trust in chariots, and some in horses;
but we will remember the name of the LORD our God.
PSALM 20:7 NKJV

This may seem like an odd prayer for a king going out to battle, but it shows where David's heart was. He knew his war equipment could fail, but God could not.

What danger can we face that God is incapable of protecting us from? None. Where have we placed our trust—in Him or in worldly defenses?

PRAYER

Battles are happening all around me—at home, at work, at church, and even internally. Every day I feel like I'm entering a war zone, Lord. But I'm happy for the reminder that I can put my trust in You no matter what I'm facing. No enemy is greater than You, Father! So let others trust in weapons. Let others trust in horses. Me? I'll remain focused on the only true source of salvation—my heavenly Father. You fight my battles for me, and You only know how to win, Lord! Together, we can face any foe head-on. I'm confident as I head into battle with You! Amen.

Day 147

NO CALL-WAITING

"Call on me and come and pray to
me, and I will listen to you."
JEREMIAH 29:12 NIV

"I will listen to you." Every woman's dream.

Jeremiah knew the importance of being listened to. He proclaimed God's message for forty years to the unhearing, unseeing, unresponsive nation of Judah. His ironic good news: God is listening!

Do you ever feel like no one's listening? The Bible says God hears us every time we utter His name. How precious we are to our Creator that He bends His omnipotent ear each time we call on Him.

PRAYER

"I just want to be heard." I'm sure we've all used those words, Lord. We don't just want our words to be heard; we want our hearts to be heard. And that's not easy in today's fast-moving society. No one seems to have time to really hear us. I've experienced this firsthand—on both sides. I'm not always a great listener, especially when I'm distracted. But You, Lord? You're the best listener of all. And You hear my heart, not just my words. Best of all, You love me, so You respond to what I've said in that gentle, tender way of Yours. How grateful I am! Amen.

Day 148

OVERCOMING THE SIN BARRIER

Godly sorrow brings repentance that leads to salvation and leaves no regret.

2 CORINTHIANS 7:10 NIV

Godly sorrow comes when we feel the pain of our own sins. As we recognize our wrongdoing and acknowledge that our actions have hurt us, others, and even the heart of God, we reach the place to do something about it. We repent, and God offers His salvation.

Has sin come between you and your Savior? Turn at once in sorrow and ask Him to make everything right in your heart and soul. You'll never be sorry you did.

PRAYER

There's a big difference between saying "I'm sorry" and truly repenting, isn't there, Lord? I've said "Sorry!" a thousand times, often not even meaning it. Speaking that word helped me over a rough patch with a friend or loved one, but in my heart I kept on going like I'd done nothing wrong. There have been other times, though, when my "Sorry" wasn't a deep enough word for the remorse I was feeling. From the depths of my soul I felt anguished over what I'd done. Yet You were there to forgive and offer me a chance to start again. What a forgiving God You are! Amen.

Day 149

JUICED

God is our refuge and strength, a very ready help in trouble.

PSALM 46:1 NASB

Remember the scene from the movie *Air Force One* when Harrison Ford, as the US president, calls for help from the belly of a terrorist-hijacked plane after much death-defying effort? Just as the crucial call is dialed, his cell phone battery dies. Can you identify? What a relief that our direct line to God—prayer—is always juiced and never needs recharging!

PRAYER

When I call, You answer, Lord. I never have to wonder if You're still on the line. You're right there and the connection is crystal clear. You hear every word, even those whispered from the depths of my pain. Best of all, You respond! You come close and rescue me, revealing Your vast love for me. And you shore up my mind and emotions, making me strong where I once felt weak. There is no one else I can call on to save me, Father. Only You. And how grateful I am for a God who genuinely sees, hears, and cares. Amen.

Day 150

CLEANSING SPIRIT

I came not to call the righteous, but sinners to repentance.
LUKE 5:32 KJV

Repentance isn't meant for "good people" who only have "tiny" sins to confess. This verse reminds us that no sin is too awful for God to hear about it. God calls all who are sinful—those who most need Him and have the most to fear from His awesome holiness. Each one of us may hesitate to confess sins and admit to wrongs that embarrass us. But we are just the ones He calls. One moment of repentance, and His Spirit cleanses our lives.

PRAYER

I know Your Word says we've all sinned, Lord. And I confess that I've sinned. . .a lot. In little ways. In big ways. In ways I've been embarrassed to confess, even. Yet You come near and tell me I'm forgiven and loved, no matter how severe my transgression. All You ask is that I repent and turn from what I've done. So today I choose to do that. All of those little things I've yet to confess? I come clean about them today, Lord. Wash them away, I pray, and make me brand new. I'm Your child, cleansed and free! Amen.

Day 151

SLIP-SLIDING AWAY

Instruct those who are rich in this present world not to. . .set their hope on the uncertainty of riches, but on God, who richly supplies us with all things to enjoy.
1 TIMOTHY 6:17 NASB

My friend Claire lived large with a millionaire husband, enormous house, designer clothes, flashy convertible, and even a cook (to my envy!). But suddenly the economy headed south, and in the twinkle of a bank vault key, she lost it all. Divorced, homeless, and bitter, Claire was forced to wait tables to pay her ill son's medical bills.

We can't depend on money, which is here today, gone tomorrow. Our hope must be fixed on our eternal God.

PRAYER

My hope is built on nothing less than You, Lord, and Your heart for me. I can't put my trust in things. I can't place it in the economy. I can't even hope in my job or my abilities, as skilled as I might feel at times. Those things could be gone in a flash. But when I put my trust in You, my provider, I can't go wrong. I'll always have everything I need as long as I keep my hope squarely in You. What an amazing supplier You are, Lord! How You love us! And how secure I feel as I rest in Your tender care. Amen.

Day 152

CHOOSE FORGIVENESS

"And if he sins against you seven times in a day, and seven times in a day returns to you, saying, 'I repent,' you shall forgive him."
LUKE 17:4 NKJV

When another offends us, do we pass on the forgiveness we have received? That's what Jesus commanded. Remembering how gracious God has been to us, we also need to show grace to those who trespass against us. As we think of our many sins that God has put behind His back, can we fail to show compassion to others?

PRAYER

I get it, Lord. I have to choose to forgive, even when I don't feel like it. And I'll be honest, I often don't feel like it. There are some people who make it harder to forgive because of the way they treat me. I'd rather go on holding them in unforgiveness. But Your Word convinces me that letting things go is better—not just for them but for me. You want me to live in the freedom that forgiveness offers. So I will choose to forgive and then reap the benefits in my life. Thank You for showing me a better way. Amen.

Day 153

DAILY DUTIES

Show love in everything you do.
1 CORINTHIANS 16:14 CEV

Sometimes we get so wrapped up in our daily to-do lists that we put our duties above people. "Leave me alone until this project is finished, kids." "Sorry, Sue, I'm too busy to have lunch." "Oh, I don't have time to talk to Mom today; I'll let the answering machine get it."

How, then, can we ever share the love of Christ with those we've shoved out of our way? People don't care how much you know until they know how much you care.

PRAYER

My goodness, life is busy, Lord! I feel like it's a never-ending cycle of stuff to do: making sure the kids are up and dressed, getting them to school, driving to work, dealing with my boss, coming home, fixing dinner, helping with homework. . .all the stuff. It's a lot. Sometimes, in the chaos of the everyday, I forget to pause and show love to those I'm interacting with. Oh, I talk to them. I just don't engage with them on a deeper level. Thank You for the reminder that my day-in, day-out interactions should be centered on You. May I always show love in all I do and say. Amen.

Day 154

AVAILABLE 24-7

"Blessed is the man to whom the L*ORD shall not impute sin."*
ROMANS 4:8 NKJV

Sin forgiven: What a wonderful thought! No longer do we need to be dragged into wrongdoing, because God has cleansed our hearts. His Spirit sweeps through us, lifting the burden of sin from our lives. Though we still fail, as long as we are in Christ, God will not hold the sin against us. Forgiveness is available 24-7 as God sends His Spirit through our lives again and again.

PRAYER

I love that I can call on You 24-7, Lord. No answering service is necessary! You're always right there, just a breath away. And I'll be honest: Sometimes my deepest, darkest hours are late at night, after the sun goes down. I find myself quiet. Alone. Thinking. Pondering all of the things I've done wrong. So I cry out—often in the wee hours of the night—and there You are! You draw close and ease my concerns, dry my eyes, and remind me that You're ready to forgive, no matter the hour. I'm so grateful, Lord! Amen.

Day 155

ONE NATION UNDER GOD

The poor are filled with hope, and injustice is silenced.
Job 5:16 CEV

"Give me your tired, your poor, your huddled masses. . ." beckons the Statue of Liberty, offering a home and freedom to hurting people. Many of our ancestors flocked to American shores that were offering freedom of worship and an end to the injustice of religious persecution. May we never forget the sacrifices they made to pursue the hope of providing their children—you and me—with a nation founded on Christian principles. Let's strive to preserve that hope for future generations.

PRAYER

Oh, how precious it is when people turn their hearts and their eyes to You, Lord! You love when the nations gather to celebrate and worship You. May we all keep our faith—as individuals and as collective citizens. Today I'm so grateful for the sacrifices of those who gave their lives for the cause of freedom. And for Jesus, who gave the ultimate sacrifice of all: His life on the cross so that all—no matter where they live—could have eternal life. What a precious gift freedom is. How I cherish it, Lord! Amen.

Day 156

RECONCILERS

God was reconciling the world to himself in Christ, not counting people's sins against them. And he has committed to us the message of reconciliation.

2 CORINTHIANS 5:19 NIV

The Lord loved you so much that He paid a huge price to draw you into His arms and make you His child. Jesus' sacrifice destroyed the sin barrier separating humanity and God. As a result, those who repent are reconciled to their holy God. But faith doesn't stop there. The Lord makes us reconcilers too as He sends us out with the message that has meant so much to us: "God loves you."

PRAYER

I love how You reconcile, Lord! You pull together people who, in the natural, would never become friends. It's miraculous, really! Best of all, You reconciled us back to You even when we had fallen so far away. You're all about patching things up! And You want me to live that way too. You love for Your kids to live in unity and to reconcile after tiffs. I know not every friendship is meant to be. There are certain people to avoid. But when reconciliation is healthy (and possible), please show me so that I can live like You and love like You. Amen.

Day 157

A STRONG TOWER

The name of the LORD is a fortified tower;
the righteous run to it and are safe.
PROVERBS 18:10 NIV

We of the twenty-first century tend to limit our references to God, but ancient Hebrew translations offer a broader perspective. There is intrinsic hope in the names of God: Elohim (Mighty One), El Olam (Everlasting God), Yahweh Yireh (The Lord Will Provide), Yahweh Shalom (The Lord Is Peace), Yahweh Tsuri (The Lord, My Rock), and Abba (Father), to name a few. Let's broaden our scope of His powerful name in our prayers today.

PRAYER

I love Your many names, Lord! No matter what I'm facing, I can call on You! When I'm ill, I cry out to my Jehovah Rapha, the Lord Who Heals. When I'm anxious, You are my Yahweh Shalom, God of Peace. When I'm feeling unsettled, You are Jehovah Tsuri, my Rock. And of course, when I'm feeling alone and scared, You are my Abba Father. I trust You as the Mighty One (Elohim), adore You as the Everlasting One (El Olam), and will always turn to You as my Father. Thank You for loving me as Your precious child! Amen.

Day 158

SAVING GRACE

Truly my soul finds rest in God; my salvation comes from him.

PSALM 62:1 NIV

At the moment you repented of your sins and asked Jesus to control your life, God saved you. But He didn't stop there. Each day of your life, He continues His saving work. He protects you, redirects you, and supplies your every need. In any trouble, rest in Him. He will not fail.

PRAYER

Grace, grace, how I need Your grace, Lord. Not just in the big moments, when I've messed up, but every moment of every day. My walk with You is a process. I learn, I make mistakes, You forgive, and I get back on the path once again. You are constantly loving me, helping me, guiding me, and showing me the way to walk with You. I rest easy knowing that You know every step of my life—the parts I've already lived and the events yet to come. Best of all, I can trust You with all of it. How I praise You! Amen.

Day 159

ALWAYS ON DUTY

He will not let your foot slip—
he who watches over you will not slumber.
PSALM 121:3 NIV

I love hiking the winding mountain paths near our remote Smoky Mountain cabin. Sometimes I get so caught up in watching hummingbirds or admiring cliffside vistas that I stumble, forgetting that inattention could be deadly. How comforting to know that our Lord is always alert as He watches over us. We don't have to worry that an important prayer will slip by while He sneezes or that He'll nap through our surgery. He's always on duty.

PRAYER

Thank You for watching over me at all times, Lord. You have the best eagle-eye vision out there! I can't even imagine all of the accidents You've kept me from over the years, but I'm grateful for Your care. You are truly always on duty. And what's more, You never get weary. I don't have to worry that You're dozing off. You're alert, perceptive, and ever-watchful, knowing the enemy is out there to trip me up. Thanks for taking such great care of me, Father. I don't take Your protection for granted! Amen.

Day 160

SHINE FOR HIM

[Jesus] gave himself for us to redeem us from all wickedness and to purify for himself a people that are his very own, eager to do what is good.

TITUS 2:14 NIV

Is there any sin from which Jesus cannot save us? No. As long as we look to Him, He will lead us into increasing and joyous holiness.

God takes sinful people and changes their lives, making them His hands and feet in an evil world. As His people draw near to Him, throwing off sin, their good works shine forth the nature of their Savior. Will you shine for Him today?

PRAYER

Purified. Transformed. Made new. These are all phrases that speak of my journey since I came to know You, Lord. You changed me then. You're changing me now. And You promise to keep that transformative power working in my life well into my future. Every day I'm becoming more like You, my Savior. Thank You for consistently working in my life. The steps I take each day draw me closer and closer to You. May Christlikeness be the desire and motivation of my heart from this day forward. Amen.

Day 161

ONE GUTSY GAL

"It could be that you were made queen for a time like this!"
ESTHER 4:14 CEV

Crowned queen after winning a beauty contest, Esther was only allowed audience with her king when summoned. A wave of his scepter would pardon her from execution, but he was a hard man—and unpredictable. When Esther learned of a plot to destroy her people, she faced a tough decision. She was the only one who could save them—at supreme risk. God had intentionally placed her in that position for that time. What is your divinely ordained position?

PRAYER

Sweet young Esther. . .new to the throne and in the most awkward position imaginable! She had to make a choice—face the potential terror of the king or cower away and let her people die. She chose the courageous route and entered the throne room. Thank goodness You saved her, Lord. You saw that precious young woman as a warrior in her own right, and You worked with her to save her people. I know You'll do the same through me, if only I place myself in a position of vulnerability. So today I choose to do just that. Use me, I pray. Amen.

Day 162

OUR PARTNER

Continue to work out your salvation with fear and trembling.

PHILIPPIANS 2:12 NIV

Salvation is hard work! Not only did it require Jesus' crucifixion for our sins, but we have a part in the effort too. We have to live out the commands in God's Word that make our faith have an impact on our world. But we need not feel discouraged, for we are not alone in the labor. God acts through us by His Spirit. What better working partner could we have than God Himself?

PRAYER

I want to live a life that's pleasing to You, Lord. I'm not working to earn my salvation. You've already saved me through Your work on the cross. But I'm working out my salvation with fear and trembling so that I can honor You in my thoughts and words and actions. I also long to live in a way that draws others to You. I know many are watching how I live, so I'll do my best to be consistent in my talk and my walk so that people get the right idea about You. Thank You for doing the hard work and for showing me how to live a consistent and holy life. Amen.

Day 163

A COOL SUMMER SHOWER

"He will renew your life and sustain you in your old age."
RUTH 4:15 NIV

Ruth's blessing of renewal is applicable to us today. *Renovatio* is Latin for "rebirth." It means casting off the old and embracing the new—a revival of spirit, a renovation of attitude. Truly it is something essential for women to espouse every day of their lives. Like the relief brought by a cool rain shower on a sizzling summer day, Ruth's hope was renewed by her Lord's touch, and ours will be too if we look to Him for daily replenishing.

PRAYER

Oh, how I love a cool shower after a hot day, Lord! There's something so refreshing about stepping under that water and letting it wash away that icky sweat. I step out of that shower feeling brand-new, completely fresh, and ready to go. I'm grateful for the spiritual showers You've rained down on me over the years—those holy moments when You poured Yourself out and turned my situation around. I found the courage to step out, to keep going, to live out Your purposes for me. You're a refreshing, renewing God, and I'm so grateful! Amen.

Day 164

SPIRITUAL TRAINING

All Scripture. . .is useful for. . .training in righteousness, so that the servant of God may be thoroughly equipped for every good work.

2 TIMOTHY 3:16–17 NIV

Did you realize that God prepares you to do good works every day of your life? Because you believe in Him, He will lead you to fulfill His purposes according to His plan for your life.

How do you start? By reading the Bible, His guidebook. There you will learn what to believe, how to treat others, and how to speak with love. Soon you'll be ready to put into action all you've learned.

PRAYER

Sometimes I feel like a soldier prepping for battle, Lord. You've enlisted me in an intense training session, it seems! But I'll do the work. I'll stay in Your Word. I'll exercise my faith. I'll keep myself nimble and ready for battle. In short, I'll do all You've required of me because I know You have great works for me to carry out and I want to be prepared. Your plan for my life is great, and the preparation for it is a critical part of the equation. Thank You for this reminder, Father! Now back to work I go! Amen.

Day 165

ZOMBIE ZONE

Be joyful in hope, patient in affliction, faithful in prayer.
ROMANS 12:12 NIV

Affliction has a tendency to suck the joy right out of our lives, leaving us stranded in the dully-funks. You know—that black hole of existence where our minds fog, emotions go numb, eyes glaze over, and we languish in a state of spiritual dullness. A spiritual zombie zone. But if we're faithful in prayer, God will be faithful to rescue us from those joy-sucking dully-funks and fill us to the brim with His abundant joy.

PRAYER

I've been in that place far too often, Lord. I get stuck in the dully-funks and nothing can pull me out. My feet are glued to the floor. (Or in many cases, my backside is glued to the sofa.) When I feel that overwhelming sense of "stuckness," moving forward feels impossible. Then You remind me that I hold the keys to my freedom. I must change my thinking. I have to offer up a positive testimony. Praise. Words of encouragement, even if they're only spoken to myself. I need to change my stinkin' thinkin'. When I do, joy floods my soul, and up I come. . .out of the dully-funks! Amen.

Day 166

SERVING OTHERS

You. . .were called to be free. But do not use your freedom to indulge the flesh; rather, serve one another humbly in love.

GALATIANS 5:13 NIV

As women, we know a lot about serving: We serve on many fronts and sometimes wonder why this is our lot. God tells us He freed us from sin not so we can do what we like but so we can share His love. If we're tempted to fulfill our own sinful desires, let's remind ourselves why we are here: We obey Jesus by doing good for others. If that's not our goal, we need redirection from Him.

PRAYER

May serving others never become a drudgery, Lord! May I always see it as an opportunity, a gift, a blessing. After all, I've been served a great many times by others, and it's only right to return the favor! I want to have the kind of heart that views service as an act of love for everyone You place in my path. Doing good brings joy, and not just to the recipient! I'm blessed when I serve others. Pure satisfaction fills my heart! Thank You for the reminder that a life of service is a life of blessing and joy, heavenly Father! Amen.

Day 167

LAUGHTER AND HOPE

A joyful heart is good medicine.
PROVERBS 17:22 NASB

Laughter is to hope as nonstick cooking spray is to a shiny new muffin tin: It keeps the goo from sticking. Once the batter of everyday responsibility hardens and adheres to our attitudes, it's awfully hard to scrape off enough crust for hope to shine through. But if we coat our day with a little laughter and the joy of the Lord, problems will slide off a lot more easily and our hope will sparkle!

PRAYER

Oh, how I love to laugh, Lord! There are days when laughter bubbles up inside of me, washing away every bit of pain and anguish. On those days, I'm so grateful for a reprieve from the ickiness of life. I can overcome it. I can rise above it. I can see over the horizon of my circumstances with an eternal perspective. That's the power of joy. So help me to live like that, I pray. May more of my days be filled with laughter and joy that spill over onto everyone I meet along the way. Amen.

Day 168

YOU'RE EQUIPPED

In Christ you have been brought to fullness.
He is the head over every power and authority.
COLOSSIANS 2:10 NIV

Do you feel incomplete or inadequate, unable to carry out the tasks God has given you? You aren't, you know, if you tap into His Spirit. God equips you to do all things in Him. If you feel overwhelmed, make sure you haven't taken on tasks rightfully belonging to someone else. God does not overload your life with busyness. He has a purpose for all He calls you to do. So be certain you're serving in the right place, doing the work He planned for you.

PRAYER

I'm guilty, Lord. Often I take on too much and then wonder why I'm feeling overwhelmed. I need to slow down and do only the things You've specifically called me to do, nothing more. When I live that way, I don't feel inadequate. I actually finish the tasks I start. Please show me which areas of my life need to be adjusted so that I can make the necessary changes. Doing just those things You want me to do will be to my benefit and also to Your glory as I free myself up to be more effective in every area of my life. Amen.

Day 169

A TWO-STRANDED ROPE

The widow who is really in need and left all alone puts her hope in God and continues night and day to pray and to ask God for help.
1 TIMOTHY 5:5 NIV

Some women feel as though they are irreparably weakened when they are widowed. Where once there were three strands of a sturdy rope (his, hers, and God's), now there are two. But those who persevere through faith and true grit say the secret is to learn to rejoice in what's left instead of lamenting what has been lost. Look forward. Move forward. Keep that two-stranded rope strong, and never lose the hope of a better tomorrow.

PRAYER

I'm hanging tight to that rope, Lord. No matter what, I won't let go. Even on the days when I feel there's a significant lack in my life, I will remind myself that You are enough. With Your hand in mine, I can go on and face my tomorrows. Today I choose to dig in my heels and meet the day with courage. I'll move forward, even when I don't feel like it. And I'll trust that You not only see all of my tomorrows but have already paved the path for me to walk them out. In other words, I can put my hope in You and be perfectly safe and secure. I choose to do just that! Amen.

Day 170

GRACE IS A GIFT

But unto every one of us is given grace according to the measure of the gift of Christ.

EPHESIANS 4:7 KJV

We don't usually think of grace as a "spiritual gift." But consider this: Grace is the basis of all the gifts God gives us. Without His gracious forgiveness, we'd have nothing spiritually. Our sins so separate us that only His forgiveness allows us to approach Him. Whether we receive a large measure of grace or a smaller one, it is the perfect gift, given by Jesus, just for us. Let's appreciate what it cost Him and walk in His grace today.

PRAYER

Today I choose to walk in Your grace, Lord. I will accept it as the gift that it is and step into it with joy in my heart. Through grace, I'm saved. Through grace, I live in peace. Through grace, I can accept and offer forgiveness. Through grace. . .everything! Grace is truly the gift that keeps on giving, no matter what I happen to be walking through. And You pour it out so freely, Lord! You give it as a gift, wrapped in ribbons of mercy and bows of love. And I accept it, knowing I can extend it to others as well. Thanks for Your grace, Lord. Amen.

Day 171

BET THE FARM

Whoever plows and threshes should be able to do so in the hope of sharing in the harvest.
1 CORINTHIANS 9:10 NIV

There's a young man who works in children's church with me who is loud, brash, impulsive, an incessant talker, and loves the Lord with all his heart. The kids think he's hilarious. I think he's obnoxious. But I must remind myself that God uses him to reach young hearts with the gospel in ways that I never could. He's a plowman and I'm a thresher, and we work together to harvest souls into God's kingdom.

PRAYER

We all play our own unique roles, don't we, Lord? I'm totally different from the woman next to me. She has her special way of doing things, and I have mine. And yet You love (and use) both of us. It's amazing to think that we can all reach our own unique audience with the gospel message, based in part on our personalities. Nothing goes to waste. So I'll do my best not to judge those who are vastly different from me. Instead, I'll see them as the precious individuals You have created them to be, and I will thank You for them! Amen.

Day 172

FOR HIS GLORY

We have different gifts, according to the grace given to each of us.

ROMANS 12:6 NIV

Your spiritual gifts are tailored especially for you. God has a purpose for your life. To help you accomplish it, He has given just the gifts you need—nothing more, nothing less. Doesn't knowing that God has gifted you in just the right way make you feel special? Thank Him for those gifts today, and use them for the glory of His kingdom and to help others.

PRAYER

You gave me exactly what I need to make an impact in this world, Lord. I'll never come up short when You're the one making provision! When I need courage, You offer courage. When I need spunk, You offer spunk. When I need quiet wisdom, You offer quiet wisdom. Situations may change and my needs might shift as a result, but ultimately I can count on You to give me exactly what I need when I need it. (You're so perceptive and kind to provide for me so well, heavenly Father!) Amen.

Day 173

THE SALVAGE MASTER

We are pressed on every side by troubles,
but we are not crushed.
2 CORINTHIANS 4:8 NLT

Many women struggle with depression at some point in their lives: postpartum, post-kids (empty nest), or anytime in between. We might feel that we're being compressed into a rock-hard cube like the product of a trash compactor. The normal details of life suddenly become perplexing and overwhelming. But God does not abandon us to the garbage dump. He is the salvage master and recycles us into sterling images of His glory.

PRAYER

I've been through so many of the "posts" already, Lord. I've somehow survived them all, but I confess, I've had my moments of depression and despair in the process. I've allowed myself to get swallowed up in those moments, becoming overwhelmed and confused. But somehow You salvage it all, even the hardest situations. I might be pressed down, but I'm not abandoned—at least not by You. So day by day I'll trust You, even when situations don't make sense. I know I can trust You to work everything out to my benefit and Your glory! Amen.

Day 174

REACH OUT

Try to excel in those [gifts] that build up the church.
1 CORINTHIANS 14:12 NIV

Paul's words to the Corinthians were meant for us too. We should build up the church, not ourselves, through our spiritual gifts. When God gave you a special combination of spiritual abilities, it wasn't to make you feel important. He designed those gifts to help you reach out to those who need to accept Him as Savior and to support other believers who share your mission to reach the world. Is that how you're using your gifts today?

PRAYER

All of the gifts You've placed inside me are for a purpose, Lord. You want me to reach others in my own unique way. Instead of comparing myself to others or wondering why I'm not gifted like they are, I'll spend more time figuring out how to use the gifts You've given me to spread the word of Your kingdom. I'll build others up so that they can come to know You as I know You. And I'll do so with joy in my heart, brimming with gratitude for the opportunity to be of service. Amen.

Day 175
LOOK TO THE SUNRISE

I rise before dawn and cry for help;
I have put my hope in your word.
PSALM 119:147 NIV

Could be stress or worry or berserk hormones. Whatever the cause, many women find themselves staring at their dark bedroom ceilings in the wee morning hours. We try counting sheep, but they morph into naughty little children, and we exhaust ourselves chasing them through fitful dreams. We're tormented by the "what-ifs," guilted by the "should haves," and jolted wider awake by the "don't forget to's." But a new day is dawning, and help is but a prayer away.

PRAYER

I want to rest easy in You, Lord, but I can't always seem to let go. Too often I let the craziness of the day spill over into the night. And sometimes, just before the alarm goes off, I find myself wide awake, stressing over the new day before it even begins. That's when I do my best to turn my thoughts to You. I cry out to You, asking for grace to face the day with peace. With hope. With joy. With enthusiasm. You give me courage to rise, face the situations in front of me, and tackle them with Your hand in mine. Thank You! Amen.

Day 176

CHRISTIAN STRENGTH

Finally, be strong in the Lord and in his mighty power.

EPHESIANS 6:10 NIV

When you rely on God's strength, what are you tapping into? Not some small pool of power that fails at a critical moment. The Christian's strength is mighty because God is mighty. He who created the universe does not have a short arm that cannot reach down to your situation. Shining stars testify to His authority. Galaxies in space are ordered by His hand. Can He not order your life too? Ask Him to pour His strength into your life, and you will have all you need.

PRAYER

You are the ultimate strength, Lord! A million iron tablets don't even come close! When I tap into Your strength, supernatural things happen. I witness miracles. I overcome obstacles. You—the one who flung the stars into space—offer the same creative power to me, Your child. Not so I can show off or prove anything special about myself, but only to show the world that You love and care for Your own. Thank You for reaching down into my crazy situations and proving Yourself time and time again. What a powerful and loving God You are! Amen.

Day 177

CHILL

I lie awake thinking of you, meditating on you through the night. Because you are my helper, I sing for joy in the shadow of your wings.

PSALM 63:6–7 NLT

Are you a worrier? Do you frequently find yourself working up a sweat building molehills into mountains during the midnight hours? This passage suggests an alternative to that nasty and unproductive habit. Instead of worrying, try meditating on the loving-kindness of God. Like a distressed chick tucked safely beneath the snug wings of the mother hen, let the joy of being loved and protected relax your tense muscles and ease you into peaceful rest.

PRAYER

What is it about the nighttime hours, Lord, that opens our hearts and minds to fretting? Is it the stillness? The solitude? Am I finally able to think more clearly, to see the problems more vividly without all of the chaos of the day swirling around me? Sometimes I think the midnight hours are both the best and worst part of the day—best because I'm finally free to lie down in the quiet of the night, and worst because the quiet is interrupted by my fears and worries. Thank You for meeting me in the midnight hour, Lord. Even then, I'm safely tucked away in Your care. Amen.

Day 178

HAVE COURAGE

Be on your guard; stand firm in the faith; be courageous; be strong.
1 CORINTHIANS 16:13 NIV

Being a Christian can take a lot of courage. As the world around us becomes increasingly hostile to God and our personal lives become tense because of our beliefs, we feel the challenge. But we are not defenseless. Christians through the ages have faced these troubles and triumphed. The Lord who supported them gives us strength too. Let us stand fast for Jesus, calling on His Spirit to shore up our lives. Then we will be strong indeed.

PRAYER

I'm going to admit something hard, Lord. I don't always have a ton of courage. I would rather hide under the covers with my fingers in my ears than listen to the roar of the storm outside. But You call me to stand, to be courageous, even when I don't feel like it. I can do so only with Your help. Thank You for the reminder that I'm not defenseless. You're the one fighting my battles. Even when the enemies of this world come against me, they're really battling You. So I will stand firm. Thanks for infusing me with Your strength. Amen.

Day 179

SHOWERS OF BLESSING

Do the skies themselves send down showers?
No, it is you, Lord our God. Therefore our hope is
in you, for you are the one who does all this.
JEREMIAH 14:22 NIV

Have you ever stood in your parched garden, praying for rain? The plants you've nurtured from seeds are wilting, flower petals litter the ground, fruit is withering on the vine. Then thunderclouds roll in and the skies burst forth with reinvigorating rain.

There will be dry times in our spiritual gardens too, but our hope is in the Lord our God, who sends showers to revive us. Deluge us today, Lord.

PRAYER

I've walked through seasons when I felt completely dried up, Lord. Parched didn't even begin to describe it. And I've skipped through other seasons when I sensed Your rain pouring down, flooding my soul and nurturing me back to health. Even in the dry seasons, I won't give up. I'll simply turn to You, the maker of the rain clouds, knowing You will send rain in due season. Pour it out, I pray! Saturate me with Your love, Your kindness, Your mercy, and Your joy. I want to live a fully soaked life. Amen.

Day 180

LIFT THEM UP!

We who are strong ought to bear with the failings of the weak and not to please ourselves.

ROMANS 15:1 NIV

No doubt God has made you strong in some area—perhaps by experience, as you have struggled to obey Him. Now, how do you respond to others? Don't criticize those who have different experiences or different strengths, and don't carp about the failings of new or weaker Christians. Instead, use your power to lift others up. Come alongside and help. Then God's strength will have helped you both.

PRAYER

There are days when I can barely lift myself up, Lord. I lean heavily on You! Then there are days when I find myself lifting up others—some quite unexpectedly! Because I've walked a mile in their shoes, I seem like the appropriate candidate to help them through their struggles. It's funny how You arrange those things. Thanks for the reminder that You often place the strong around us when we're weak. And when no one happens to be around? Well, You're always with us, and You're the strongest one of all! Amen.

Day 181

SNIPPETS OF HOPE

I also pray that you will understand the incredible greatness of God's power for us who believe him.

EPHESIANS 1:19 NLT

Daydreams are snippets of hope for our souls. Yearnings for something better, something more exciting, something that will lift our spirits. Some dreams are mere fancy, but others are meant to last a lifetime because God has embedded them in our hearts. It's when we lose sight of those dreams that hope dies.

But God offers us access to His almighty power—the very same power that brought His Son back from the dead. What greater hope could there be?

PRAYER

I love when You give me little glimmers of hope, Lord. Those fun daydreams are the best! I can see myself doing great things with Your help. Of course, not every dream is meant to come true—I know that. But that doesn't make the dreaming any less adventurous! Thanks for always giving me hope even when the situations around me are bleak. Those snippet-dreams keep me going and flood me with joy. And who knows? With Your help I just might accomplish many of them! Here's hoping, Lord! Amen.

Day 182

MAKE THE MOST

Since everything will be destroyed in this way, what kind of people ought you to be? You ought to live holy and godly lives.

2 PETER 3:11 NIV

Knowing that the world will not last forever, how should we act? We have no devil-may-care option, in which we act as if eternity doesn't matter, because God calls us to live wholly for Him. The world's coming destruction should not make us careless but rather vigilant to make the most of our time. In the end, all we do here will not be lost but will pass on into eternity.

PRAYER

I long to make the most of every single minute of every single day, Lord. I don't want to waste a nanosecond! I've lived long enough to understand that this life is fleeting. We're not guaranteed our next breath. But we're already pointed in the direction of eternity. Our feet are halfway to heaven already. So what's the point in holding back? No, I want to be known as a woman who lived with her whole heart, eager to face the challenges of each new day and happy for the breath in her lungs. Thanks for this amazing life! Amen.

Day 183

TRUE SUCCESS

"For I know the plans I have for you,"
declares the Lord, *"plans to prosper you. . . ,*
plans to give you hope and a future."
Jeremiah 29:11 NIV

As little girls, we dream about the handsome man we'll marry one day, exciting trips we'll take, the mansion we'll call home, and the beautiful, perfect children we'll have. A successful life—isn't that what we hope for?

But God doesn't call us to be successful; He calls us to trust Him. We may never be successful in the world's eyes, but trust in our Father's omnipotence ensures our future and our hope. And that's true success.

PRAYER

Sometimes I focus too much on the dream life and not the holy life You've planned for me. I see myself with the white picket fence, a houseful of kids, a husband who adores me, and plenty of money in the bank. I don't plan for the days when I don't feel like crawling out of bed in the morning or when those kids come down with the flu. Turns out, life is a lot harder than I imagined. (Go figure!) But You want me to reanalyze my definition of success, so I'll start by thanking You for the life I already have. May I live it to honor You! Amen.

Day 184

YOU HAVE GIFTS!

Now to each one the manifestation of the Spirit is given for the common good.

1 CORINTHIANS 12:7 NIV

Did you know that you are a gifted person? God gives each of His children spiritual gifts designed to help themselves and others—wisdom, knowledge, faith, healing, to name just a few. As you grow spiritually, you begin to unwrap these presents from God. Over time, you may be surprised and blessed by how many He has provided for you.

Feeling unimportant? Remind yourself that you're gifted by God!

PRAYER

I don't always feel very gifted, Lord. It seems kind of weird to say, "God has given me special gifts and abilities." But You have! You've given me wisdom, knowledge, faith, and so much more! And Your intention for those gifts is good—so that I will reach others with the gospel message. So I'll take the gifts You've placed inside of me, both small and large, and use them for You. I won't hesitate to share my faith with others so that they can come to know You too. Thanks for gifting me, Lord. Amen.

Day 185

YOU CAN'T LOSE

Alive, I'm Christ's messenger; dead, I'm his prize. Life versus even more life! I can't lose.

PHILIPPIANS 1:21 MSG

The old-timer smiled at his granddaughter as she rebuked him for driving the farm tractor. "Don't you know the danger at your age, Grandpa? You could be killed!"

"I'm not worried, darlin', and you shouldn't be either. What's the worst that could happen? I wake up in heaven. This life versus an even better one. . .for all eternity."

When worry begins to overshadow hope, remember three little words from Philippians: I can't lose!

PRAYER

The older I get, the dearer heaven seems, Lord. As a little child I didn't feel that way, if I'm being honest. Back then I wanted to live here on earth forever. Death seemed terrifying! But now that I have a few years under my belt, I see that heaven is waiting with open arms. And I already have so many friends and loved ones waiting for me there. I can only imagine how glorious it will be to be reunited with them in Your presence, to walk on streets of gold, and to share eternity with a never-ending song of praise on my lips! What a day that will be! Amen.

Day 186

ETERNAL BLESSINGS

A faithful man will abound with blessings,
but he who hastens to be rich will not go unpunished.
PROVERBS 28:20 NKJV

Faithfulness to God or success in the world: Have you had to choose between them? Seeking the world's goals brings short-term benefits, but only God provides abundant and ongoing blessings for those who put serving Him first in their lives. Though worldly blessings last for a day, a year, or a few years, they cannot remain for eternity. When you consider success, think of the kind that really lasts.

PRAYER

I'm learning what it means to be faithful to You, Lord. None of this "be true to yourself" stuff for me. No, I've been there, done that. I lived for myself for years and it didn't work out. In Your Word, You've shown me a better way to live, and I want to embrace it! I want to please Your heart, because when I do, my own heart will be happy and content. So I'll be faithful to You, knowing that when I lean in to Your way of living, I'll be successful in every area of my life. The world might not see it that way, but You do! And it's Your heart I want to please. Amen.

Day 187

EASY AS ABC

God has done all this, so that we will look for him and reach out and find him. He isn't far from any of us.

Acts 17:27 CEV

God is near, but we must reach out for Him. There's a line that we choose to cross, a specific action we take. We can't wander into the kingdom of God; it's an intentional decision. It's simple, really—as simple as ABC. A is Admitting we're sinful and in need of a Savior. B is Believing that Jesus died for our sins and rose from the grave. C is Committing our lives to Him. Life everlasting is then ours.

PRAYER

Thank You for giving us access to heaven through Your Son, Lord God! I'm so grateful for the opportunity to say yes to Jesus' work on the cross! When I admitted my sinful state, believed in Your gift of salvation, and committed my life to serving You forever, everything changed! What a difference those three little ABCs made—they (literally) transformed my whole life! May I share that simple but profound message with all I meet, Lord. Thank You for drawing near to us and offering us eternal life. Amen.

Day 188

LIVING IN HIM

The meek will inherit the land and enjoy peace and prosperity.
PSALM 37:11 NIV

You might call this God's definition of success: a profitable land that provides for His people and His peace that provides a blessed life. Notice that money and other possessions aren't mentioned. But the peace of living in Him flows freely to those who abide in Him. Would this be success to you? If not, what does that tell you about your spiritual life?

PRAYER

I want to be spiritually successful, Lord, and that means I have to humble myself and live a peaceful life. I don't always strive for peace. Sometimes I enjoy stirring things up, especially during election years. But You want me to abide in You, to trust You, and to live a life that doesn't lash out at others. I can only have peace with others if I'm at peace in my heart with You. So please quiet my heart today. Wash away any angst or frustration. And lead me back to green pastures and quiet waters, where I can rest with You. Amen.

Day 189

BESTSELLER

The mystery is that Christ lives in you,
and he is your hope of sharing in God's glory.
COLOSSIANS 1:27 CEV

Everybody loves a good mystery—as long as the plot twists a bit and the good guy wins in the end. The Christian life is a mystery. It's baffling that God could love us so deeply that He sent His only Son to suffer and die for us. And now the risen Christ lives in our hearts, bridging the gap between us and God forever. What an incredible page-turner!

PRAYER

My life has had so many twists and turns, Lord! I can barely keep up. At times it really is a bit like a mystery, complete with good guys and bad guys, sleuths, and red herrings! I find myself confused and torn. But You always know what's happening. You have everything under control at all times, even when it feels otherwise. Thank You for coming to live inside of me and for making my story so much fun. You're the best author of all, even when those unexpected plot twists come! Amen.

Day 190

ASK JESUS

Because he himself suffered when he was tempted,
he is able to help those who are being tempted.
HEBREWS 2:18 NIV

Why can Jesus help us when temptation strikes? Because He has walked a mile in our shoes. He knows how strongly sin attracts us. But because He never fell prey to it, He can effectively show us how to resist even the strongest enticement. The biggest mistakes we make are not calling on Him and not persistently seeking His powerful aid when Satan repeatedly lures us into sin. Need help? Just ask Jesus.

PRAYER

I don't know how You did it, Jesus! You looked sin and temptation in the eye and said, "Nope. Not going there." During Your trek here on earth You lived a blameless life. I try so hard to follow Your example, but I fall short every time. Thank You for Your grace and forgiveness! I'm so grateful for the many times You've dusted me off and set me back on a good path once again. You understand my temptations and You love me through them. How very grateful I am! Amen.

Day 191

SURVIVOR

The terrible storm raged for many days. . .
until at last all hope was gone.
ACTS 27:20 NLT

Following a lovely renewal of our wedding vows on our tenth anniversary, my husband and I boarded a Caribbean cruise ship. Tragically, Hurricane Gilbert obliterated our destination, Cancun, before hurling our ship back and forth on twelve-foot waves for four interminable days. I felt hopeless, sick as a pup, and at the mercy of the storm.

Life is like that, isn't it? Unexpected storms blow up, blot out the light, and toss us about. But we are survivors!

PRAYER

Sometimes I feel like the storms won't ever stop raging, Lord. They blast in with so much force I can barely stand. But I know the one who owns the storms, the only one who can make them simmer down. So I'll stick close to You. Even if the ship is tipping. Even if the winds are howling. Even if the lightning strikes feel like they're going to set my hair on fire. There's truly no safer place to be than in the very eye of the storm, my safe space with You. Thank You for that reminder today, Father. Amen.

Day 192

GOD'S PROTECTION

The Lord knows how to deliver the godly out of temptations and to reserve the unjust under punishment for the day of judgment.

2 PETER 2:9 NKJV

Feeling surrounded by temptations? God hasn't forgotten you. He knows how to protect His children from harm and offers His wisdom to His children. Maybe you need to avoid places that could lead you into sin—that may mean taking action to find a new job or new friends. When God is trying to protect you, don't resist. Sin is never better than knowing Him.

PRAYER

I'm so grateful for your wisdom and discernment, Lord. They keep me from walking into situations I need to avoid. When I get that little nudge from the Holy Spirit, it's like a finger wagging in my face and a voice saying, "Nope! Don't go there." I might be tempted in the natural, but my spirit hears, "Danger! Danger! Danger!" So I avoid the temptation to do the wrong thing and stick with my spiritual gut. Thanks for offering these spiritual nudges, Father. You're so good at protecting Your kids! Amen.

Day 193

PRUNE JUICE, ANYONE?

Therefore, with minds that are alert and fully sober, set your hope on the grace to be brought to you when Jesus Christ is revealed.

1 PETER 1:13 NIV

Diets are demanding. They exclude chocolate éclairs and hinge on effective use of that dreaded S-word: self-control. In the fruit bowl of the Spirit, self-control is the prune. It's hard to swallow but nonetheless essential to our faith—especially where hope is concerned. If self-control isn't exercised, we can find our spirits rising and falling faster than the numbers on our bathroom scales. Like the consumption of prunes, daily use of self-control regulates us and prepares us for action.

PRAYER

I'll be honest, Lord—I don't always exhibit self-control. In fact, there are days when I lose control completely. My diet goes haywire. My temper flares. My emotions get the best of me. On those days, I don't have to wonder why people back away from me. I would avoid me too if I could. But then You manage to calm me down in that amazing way You have. You remind me that I'm created in Your image and that You exhibited self-control when it came to punishing me for my sins. You give me a hug and say, "You can do better tomorrow, kid." And I do. Amen.

Day 194

GIVE THANKS

Give thanks to the God of gods. His love endures forever.
PSALM 136:2 NIV

Having trouble being thankful? Read Psalm 136. You'll be reminded of the wonders of God's power and of His enduring love. The God who protected Israel watches over you too. Even when there may be little in your life to rejoice about, you can always delight in Him. Give thanks to God. He has not forgotten you—His love endures forever.

PRAYER

I have a great many things to be thankful for, Lord. My salvation. My relationship with You. My health. My family. My friends. My income. A roof over my head. Food in my stomach. Hope for tomorrow. Peace for today. A beautiful sunset. Air flowing in and out of my lungs. On and on the blessings go. And though I don't always pause to say, "Thank You," right now I choose to do so. You are the lover of my soul and the giver of each and every blessing. May I always honor and praise You for the way You care for Your own. Amen.

Day 195

TRUE COLORS

May integrity and honesty protect me,
for I put my hope in you.
PSALM 25:21 NLT

At first the raven appeared solid black, but when she perched in a shaft of sunlight, her feathers shimmered in iridescent emerald, turquoise, and teal—her true colors.

We sometimes hide little acts of dishonesty—taking the bank's pen, pocketing that extra dollar from the clerk's mistake, fudging tax figures. But our integrity is on display at all times to the one who gave His life for us. When our true colors are exposed in the Son-light, we want to shimmer too.

PRAYER

It's the little things, isn't it, Lord? The tiny acts of dishonesty are huge to You. Oh, I try to tuck them away, but You still see. Even if others don't know, You do. Today I ask You to stir my heart to see that these little indiscretions are actually big ones, worthy of acknowledging and repenting of. I want to live a life that is pleasing to You—in big ways and in small ones. So no more tiny slips for me. I'll do my best to shine a light on the places I've kept hidden in the dark and to be honest with You and myself. Amen.

Day 196

GOD SAVES

I will give you thanks, for you answered me; you have become my salvation.

PSALM 118:21 NIV

A new believer didn't write this verse. The psalmist doesn't just thank God for loving him enough to snatch him from the claws of original sin; instead, this mature man of faith recognizes that God saves him every day, whenever he is in trouble. God does regular rescue work in your life too. What saving acts has He performed in your life recently? What thanks do you need to offer Him now?

PRAYER

I'm so glad You're in the saving business, Lord. You didn't just save me from eternal damnation; You've saved me from a thousand other snares as well. Such as my pride. My temper. Temptations. And so on. You've saved me from accidents (whew, I've had a lot of close calls!). You've saved me from relationships I never should have entered into. And You're saving me even now from internal wranglings—the ones where I beat myself up for thinking I'm not enough. Thank You for the gift of salvation that keeps on giving! Amen.

Day 197

CREATING A CHALICE

We live by faith, not by sight.

2 CORINTHIANS 5:7 NIV

Okay, so you popped a tire and the boss exploded because you were late for work again. Your dog upchucked in front of the dinner guests. Your daughter failed the big test. Your elderly mother fell and broke her hip. Bill collectors recite your number by heart. That's the outside. On the inside, God is sanding your sharp edges—impatience, frustration, worry—into a smooth chalice filled with His grace.

PRAYER

It's a good thing I don't have to live by what I can see, Lord. What I see isn't always positive or encouraging. In fact, it's often pretty chaotic. Things go wrong, one after the other, and sometimes my internal angst kicks in, which only makes things worse. Thank You for the reminder that You're sanding my sharp edges. You're taking my worries, my frustrations, and my impatience, and smoothing them out. (I need a lot of smoothing, if I'm being honest.) I'm so grateful for Your patience with me, Father. Amen.

Day 198

ETERNAL APPRECIATION

Lord my God, I will praise you forever.
Psalm 30:12 NIV

Even in eternity we will be thanking God. As believers, we'll never stop appreciating God's mercy. Without His grace, we would be forever separated from Him, lost in the cares of sin and a hellish existence. The bliss of a heavenly eternity could not be our inheritance.

Could you thank Jesus too much now? Or could you ever find enough words to show Him your love? Maybe it's time to get started on your eternal appreciation of your Lord.

PRAYER

Morning, noon, and night, Lord. . .I praise You. I thank You for reaching down through space and time and coming to this planet to connect with the people You created—not just now but for all eternity. Thank You for showing us how to live and for offering the ultimate sacrifice: Your life. Thank You that even in Your hardest moments, You went right on teaching us how to live and how to give. Most of all, thank You for the love You poured out then and are still pouring out now. If not for Your love, I truly don't know where I would be! Amen.

Day 199

A LIFE OF INTEGRITY

"Is your fear of God not your confidence,
and the integrity of your ways your hope?"
JOB 4:6 NASB

"Live your faith." These three little words are the goal of every Christian. Not "Don't smoke, cuss, or chew or hang around with those who do," or even "Be good so you'll get into heaven." Integrity begets good behavior, not the other way around. We want to please our Lord through righteous behavior so we can fulfill this challenge: "Preach the gospel at all times. Use words if necessary."

PRAYER

I want to please Your heart from the inside out, Lord! I know You're looking for genuine love and obedience, not just rule-following born of necessity. I want to be known as a woman of integrity, one who truly lives out what she believes. I want to be able to say that my life was a sermon, a gospel message that attracted even strangers to a relationship with You. Living my faith out loud is the only way. Thank You for using me to preach the finest message of all, the story of Your love. Amen.

Day 200

LOOK AHEAD TO HEAVEN

For our light and momentary troubles are achieving for us an eternal glory that far outweighs them all.

2 CORINTHIANS 4:17 NIV

What trouble could you face on earth that will not seem small in heaven? No pain from this life will impede you there. Blessing for faithful service to God will replace each heartache that discourages you today. When trials and troubles beset you, look ahead to heaven. Jesus promises you an eternal reward if you keep your eyes on Him.

PRAYER

It's remarkable to realize there will be no woes in heaven. No problems. No stumbling blocks. No tempers. No tears. I won't have to worry about what others think of me or whether I've done a good enough job on a project. There won't be any broken hearts, regrets, or shame. No, when I dwell with You eternally in heaven, there will only be bliss, Jesus. All of the pain of this life will be behind me. So I'll go ahead and start focusing on the glories of heaven now. What would be the point in waiting when I can have heaven in my heart and mind today? Amen.

Day 201

MEET ME THERE

Christ gives me the strength to face anything.

PHILIPPIANS 4:13 CEV

Most women dread going out alone—to restaurants, stores, social events, even church. Sometimes we are the loneliest when we're in a crowd. It's intimidating to face a roomful of strangers. But it's well worth it to bite the bullet and just go to that church brunch or spiritual retreat or Bible study. I would have missed some awesome blessings if I hadn't gone (alone) to different spiritual events throughout the years. I found I did know somebody after all. Jesus met me there.

PRAYER

Being alone can feel awkward. Weird. But I know I'm never truly alone, Lord, because You're always with me. So the next time I have the opportunity to go somewhere all by my lonesome, I'll remind myself of that. I won't worry about bumping up against strangers because You'll give me everything I need to make it through the event just fine. I don't want to miss out on what You have for me, so I'll muster up the courage to do brave things. Thanks for always sticking with me, Lord. I'm so grateful to never be alone. Amen.

Day 202

JOY IS STRAIGHT AHEAD

The genuineness of your faith, being much more precious than gold that perishes, though it is tested by fire, may be found to praise, honor, and glory at the revelation of Jesus Christ.

1 PETER 1:7 NKJV

Trials have a purpose in our lives. As a smith heats up gold to purify it, God heats up our lives to make spiritual impurities rise to the surface. If we cooperate with Him, sin is skimmed off our lives, purifying our faith. Cleansed lives bring glory to God and joy to us. If a trial lies before you today, envision the joy ahead.

PRAYER

I feel as if I've been purified in the fire way too many times to count, Lord. Isn't all of the dross off me yet? Still, I'm grateful that You have a purpose for each and every trial. You're getting rid of the things that weigh me down, replacing them with pure gold. (And I've always been a fan of gold.) So do Your work, Lord. Purify me. Cleanse me from within. Do all that it takes to make me like Christ. I want to be holy—truly holy. And if that means a little time in the fire, well, so be it! Amen.

Day 203

FLY ME AWAY

But those who hope in the Lord *will renew their strength. They will soar on wings like eagles; they will run and not grow weary, they will walk and not be faint.*

Isaiah 40:31 NIV

On those weary days when our chins drag on the ground, when our feet are stuck fast in the quagmire of everyday responsibilities, this verse becomes our hope and our prayer: May I mount up with wings like eagles, Father, and fly away! Let my spirit soar above the clouds on the currents of Your strength. Make me as strong as a marathon runner, continuing mile after mile after mile. Be my tailwind, Lord. Amen.

PRAYER

Oh, if only, Lord! If only I could fly with the wings of an eagle, far above my circumstances and pain. But wait! Your Word says I can do exactly that. I can rise above it all, wings outstretched, and take to the skies, my troubles tucked beneath me as I soar into the headwinds. I don't have to be stuck in the quagmire. I don't have to let the daily drudgery get me down. I can fly above the humdrumness and elevate my heart, my thinking, and my attitude. Thanks for giving me wings to soar, Lord! Amen.

Day 204
GREATER WAYS

For since, in the wisdom of God, the world through wisdom did not know God, it pleased God through the foolishness of the message preached to save those who believe.
1 CORINTHIANS 1:21 NKJV

To this world, God's wisdom doesn't look very wise. Yet anyone who denies Jesus is blind to the depth of insight God showed in sending His Son to die for us and then raising Him from the dead. Those who accept His sacrifice understand that God's ways are greater than ours and His astuteness far outweighs our own. As His wisdom fills our once-foolish lives, we gain a new perspective on His perception.

PRAYER

The world can't seem to figure You out, Lord. Your ways are definitely different, that's for sure! Sending Your Son to die for humankind? Who can fathom such a thing? And yet that's exactly what You did. Your ways are greater. Your thoughts are higher. Your plan is so far above anything we could think of, it will never make sense to the human mind. And that's exactly what makes it all so remarkable! You—the awesome creator of everything—want to include us in this amazing plan! May I always choose Your ways above my own, Lord! Amen.

Day 205

REBOOT

Be strong in the Lord and in his mighty power.
EPHESIANS 6:10 NLT

The toilet overflows, check bounces, temper flares, scale shows a three-pound gain, kids stampede, husband forgets again. . .

Ever have one of those days? How marvelous that when we're at our weakest point, our Lord is at His strongest—and He gladly shares His strength with us. He won't necessarily fix the plumbing, but He will reboot our attitude.

PRAYER

Is it possible to be strong and weak at the same time, Lord? When things are crashing down around me and I feel like someone has pulled the plug on my "want to". . .that's when You ask me to feel strong in You? Clearly it's all on You, because I'm a hot mess in moments like those! Yet You sweep in and make things better, even when a situation feels impossible. You prove Yourself strongest when I'm at my very weakest. And even though my circumstances don't always change, I'm able to get through them, reenergized by You. Thank You, Lord! Amen.

Day 206

WISE HUMILITY

Woe unto them that are wise in their own eyes, and prudent in their own sight!

Isaiah 5:21 KJV

Wisdom without humility isn't wisdom at all. When we feel astute under our own power, we're actually in big trouble and heading into foolishness! The truly wise person recognizes that all wisdom comes from God, not from frail humans. As we seek His heart and mind on every issue we encounter, we are wise indeed. No one is wiser than He is.

PRAYER

Sometimes I think I'm "all that and a bag of chips," Lord. I get a little too puffed up. I start to look at my accomplishments, my particular gifts and talents, and see myself as something more than what I am—a flawed human in need of Your mercy, grace, and assistance. Thank You for the reminder that all I am, all I will ever be, is Your child. Any wisdom or ability I have comes straight from You. Without You, I'm nothing. Today I acknowledge this truth and lean on You as my sole support. Amen.

Day 207

FEARFULLY MADE

You knit me together in my mother's womb. I praise you because I am fearfully and wonderfully made.

PSALM 139:13–14 NIV

Crow's-feet, frizzy hair, saddlebags, big feet—most women dislike something about their bodies. We feel much more fearfully than wonderfully made. But God loves us just as we are. He wants us to look past the wrinkles and see laugh footprints, to use those knobby knees for praying and those age-spotted hands for serving. And in the process, we can praise Him for limbs that move, eyes that see, and ears that hear His Word.

PRAYER

Oh, those imperfections! They stare at me in the mirror, Lord. I cringe as I see another wrinkle, another flab roll, another gray hair. But You're not flinching at all, are You? You're looking at me—Your child, Your creation—and smiling with delight. In fact, You're singing and dancing over me. I'll join the dance too, with my knobby knees and wrinkly elbows. You don't care about all of that, so why should I let it bother me? Thank You for the reminder that You see me as Your beautiful child, Lord. Amen.

Day 208

WISE WORDS

She speaks with wisdom, and faithful
instruction is on her tongue.
PROVERBS 31:26 NIV

The virtuous woman's mouth speaks kindly wisdom. Hers is no sharp tongue that destroys relationships. As we seek to do God's will, truthful yet caring speech must be ours. Wise words heal hurting hearts. If we have trouble knowing what words will bring God's healing, we need only ask Him to let His Spirit bring wisdom and kindness to our lips. When we speak as His Spirit directs, we are wise indeed.

PRAYER

I want to walk so closely with You, Lord, that Your words are on the tip of my tongue at all times, even when I'm having a rough day. Flood my heart and mind with Your wisdom, Your peace, and Your kindness. Direct every word that comes out of my mouth. May I shine like a bright light, pointing others to the truth of Your Word. When people mention my name after I'm long gone, may they add the words, "I never heard her say a cross word about anyone." I want to be known as a woman whose wise words heal hearts. Amen.

Day 209

SEND ME A SIGN

Let your unfailing love surround us, Lord,
for our hope is in you alone.
Psalm 33:22 NLT

With deadlines and schedules swirling in my head while driving down the interstate, I did a double take at the car passing me. A white-painted message across the back passenger window grabbed my attention: I AM LOVED. Wow. So am I. It only took a moment to thank Papa God for His unfailing love, but a smile lit my face all day. A simple but profound reminder is all we need from time to time.

PRAYER

I love the little reminders of Your love, Lord! I see them every day. The rising sun cries out, "He loves you so much that He's giving you another day to enjoy His goodness!" A baby's smile reminds me of the innocence and joy of life. And the twinkle in the eye of that elderly woman in line behind me at the grocery store? She definitely radiates Your love to all who come in contact with her. May I never miss the signs of Your love as they pass me by each day, Lord. What a wonderful Father You are! Amen.

Day 210

SHARE HIS LOVE

I pray that your partnership with us in the faith may be effective in deepening your understanding of every good thing we share for the sake of Christ.

PHILEMON 1:6 NIV

Many of us have a hard time sharing our faith. So when we hear Paul's encouragement to Philemon, we feel our hearts lift, knowing we aren't the only ones who struggle. Isn't the challenge of witnessing to others worth it once we've read this promise? The salvation of others and our own appreciation of our Lord—could we have better reasons to share His love?

PRAYER

I'm doing my best to share my faith with others, Lord. I used to worry that I wasn't qualified to do so. But then I realized it is as simple as just living out my faith in front of a watching world. Sharing as opportunities arise. Loving people. Responding appropriately to situations. Your Word says others will know we are Christians by our love, and I'm learning that's true! When I treat people the way You want me to treat them, they get a full dose of the gospel message. And I don't even have to preach a sermon! Thanks for that reminder, Lord. Amen.

Day 211

NO GREATER COMFORT

"O death, where is your victory? O death, where is your sting?"
1 CORINTHIANS 15:55 NLT

There's no denying that the loss of a loved one stings. Our hearts ache with pain. But Christ's victory over death after His crucifixion enables His followers to experience that same victory. We, too, will stand as conquerors of the grave, arm in arm with believers who have gone before us. What greater hope? What greater comfort?

PRAYER

"O death, where is your victory?" I've cried out these words after losing a loved one, Lord. I've felt the sting of death, and it hurts. A lot. There were nights of gut-wrenching loss and pain, and mornings when I didn't want to get out of bed. But when I view death as a transition from this life to life eternal, it lessens the sting. I see the truth staring me in the face. Eternal life is ours for the taking. My loved ones are already experiencing the joy of heaven even now. And one day I will join them, victorious over death and the grave. Amen.

Day 212

SHINE ON

"You are the light of the world.
A town built on a hill cannot be hidden."
MATTHEW 5:14 NIV

God intends for you to be a light set where the world can see it clearly—not a flame hidden behind closed doors, with curtains drawn. Being a light isn't always easy. People see everything you do, and they don't always like it. Don't let the critics stop you. Your works were ordained to glorify God, not to make people comfortable. Knowing that, are you ready to shine today?

PRAYER

Some folks might say I shine a little too bright at times, Lord. But (I must confess) I'm often pointing the spotlight on myself, not You. Thank You for the reminder that my light is on display and people are watching, even when I don't realize it. You want me to go on shining, so I will do my best to glorify You, not myself. I won't hide my light under a bushel. I'm like a town built on a hill, a light shimmering brightly to draw my friends, neighbors, and coworkers to You, Jesus. So I'll shine bright! Amen.

Day 213

LAUGH A RAINBOW

"When I see the rainbow in the clouds,
I will remember the eternal covenant between
God and every living creature on earth."
GENESIS 9:16 NLT

Ever feel like a cloud is hanging over your head? Sometimes the cloud darkens to the color of bruises, and we're deluged with a cold rain that seems to have no end. When you're in the midst of one of life's thunderstorms, tape this saying to your mirror: Cry a river, laugh a rainbow. The rainbow, the symbol of hope that God gave Noah after the flood, reminds us even today that every storm will eventually pass.

PRAYER

Cry a river, laugh a rainbow! That's going to be my motto from now on, Lord! I'm done with the woe-is-me phase of my life and I'm ready for rainbows of hope! You never meant for me to live in the doldrums. You've always been a God of hopefulness. Sure, storms will come. I've experienced a few, so I know what they feel like. But You won't let me drown. That storm will pass right over and I'll go on, eyes pointed forward, knowing that the days ahead are going to be bright and sunny. Thanks for reminding me of Your promises, Lord! Amen.

Day 214

KIND WORDS

Let your speech always be with grace, seasoned with salt, that you may know how you ought to answer each one.

COLOSSIANS 4:6 NKJV

Your words are a vital part of your witness. Speak to an unbeliever ungraciously, and chances are good she will never forget it. But study and grow in the Word, and then speak wisely and graciously to others, and God can use your words to win them to His kingdom. People respond well to kindness and flavorful speech. What are your words saying today?

PRAYER

Sometimes my words are a little too salty, Lord. I kick back with a reaction before thinking it through. Oops! I've regretted those sharp responses many times, but once the words are out of my mouth, there's no taking them back. I simply have to commit to do better next time. I'm definitely going to try harder to be a reflection of You in all I say and do. Thank You for the reminder that my words matter. I can win people to Your kingdom with sweet, kind words. Help me to remember that in the moment so that I draw people to You. Amen.

Day 215

ASKING WHY?

But God will never forget the needy;
the hope of the afflicted will never perish.
PSALM 9:18 NIV

Why me? Why is God allowing this to happen? Why doesn't He intervene?

When we're in the midst of a difficult time, it's easy to forget that God is not the afflicter, but rather is the helper and healer of the afflicted. He is not cracking the whip but feels every stripe inflicted on our backs by a sin-filled world—just like those inflicted on His only Son, Jesus.

PRAYER

There's not a thing I could go through that You wouldn't understand, Lord. You feel my every pain and see every single tear. I'm sorry for the times I got angry with You when things didn't go my way. I don't always remember that You are for me, not against me. You're not the one inflicting the pain. You're the one drying my tears and wrapping me in Your gentle embrace. Sometimes (just being honest) I forget we're in this together. You're not out to get me. In fact, You love me so much that You will never leave me or forsake me. Thank You, Lord. Amen.

Day 216

TURN FROM WRONG

There is therefore now no condemnation to those who are in Christ Jesus, who do not walk according to the flesh, but according to the Spirit.

ROMANS 8:1 NKJV

No condemnation! What a wonderful thought for sinners! Forgiven, we know the comfort of having heaven as our ultimate destination. But have we also read the second part of the verse? This is no blanket agreement that okays sin. The joy of our freedom must lead us to turn from all wrong. Our Lord gives the strength to grow in Him.

PRAYER

Sometimes I feel like I'm in a court of law, Lord, and I set myself up as judge and jury. I come down hard—on myself and others. (Why do I do that? It never ends well!) Help me realize that You came to set me free from condemnation. Now that I'm walking in relationship with You, I don't have to go on beating myself up. You've forgiven me, given me the opportunity to begin again. You're all about fresh starts. I've turned away from sin and I'm embracing this new life with You. Thanks for making all things new, Lord! Amen.

Day 217

TUNE IN

And hope does not put us to shame, because God's love has been poured out into our hearts through the Holy Spirit, who has been given to us.

ROMANS 5:5 NIV

Is your spiritual antenna tuned in to the Holy Spirit? The Holy Spirit is the communicator of the Trinity: our helper, comforter, and instructor. Through Him, God pours love and hope into us. Like radio waves broadcasting invisibly through the atmosphere, the Holy Spirit communicates to believers. We must, however, make the effort to tune in our receivers to His frequency and then choose to obey His guidance—even when it's inconvenient.

PRAYER

I'm tuned in, Lord! I want to hear every word You have for me. I don't want to miss a thing! It's so remarkable to realize You're still speaking to Your kids today. We simply have to listen. Through the sweet, tender voice of Your Holy Spirit, I'm given instruction, power, comfort, and guidance to know just what to do—in good times and in bad. So I'll lean in close. I'll keep my eyes and ears wide open for Your instruction, and then I'll follow through and do what You say. Antenna up! Amen.

Day 218

INHERITORS OF EARTH

"Blessed are the meek, for they will inherit the earth."
MATTHEW 5:5 NIV

In the workplace, meekness isn't often seen as a positive thing. "Looking out for number one" is the theory of many who tout assertiveness as the way to get the most out of life.

But God doesn't say that. Ultimately, those who follow Him faithfully and show their belief to the world will not be the "nice guys" who "finish last," but the inheritors of this earth. What plot of earth might God have mapped out for you?

PRAYER

Your ways are so different from the ways of this world, Lord. Sometimes it's confusing. I buy into the whole "Work your way to the top rung of the ladder no matter what it takes" mentality. I forget to be humble. I don't remember that the meek will inherit the earth. I just dive right in, clawing my way to the top. But that never really works out, does it? Your ways are higher. Your ways—though they might not make sense in the here and now—will yield the ultimate payout in the end. So I'll keep doing things Your way, Lord. Amen.

Day 219

SAINTS PRESERVE US

I will always praise you in the presence of your faithful people.

PSALM 52:9 NIV

We sing, "Lord, I want to be in that number, when the saints go marching in!" But who exactly are saints? Exceptionally good people like Saint Nicholas or Mother Teresa? The Bible calls all true believers saints. Some think if their derriere simply graces a pew, they're in. But sitting in church no more makes you a Christian than standing in your closet makes you a vacuum cleaner. Only dedicated Christ lovers will march into heaven. Are you in that number?

PRAYER

I hardly think of myself as a saint, Lord. Yet that's what Your Word says I am. All believers are "saints," even those of us who sin and fall short. I love that You see us all as one big family, unlimited by time or location. I have saintly brothers and sisters all over the globe. And those who've gone before us, the ones who gave their lives to You dozens—or even hundreds—of years ago? They're part of the family too! And one day we'll all live together in heaven with You, Lord. What a glorious day that will be! Amen.

Day 220

EVERYTHING FOR GOD

Whatever you do, work at it with all your heart, as working for the Lord.
COLOSSIANS 3:23 NIV

Did you know you are not really working for your boss? Yes, you report to whoever your company hired for that position, but ultimately you do everything for God, not for a man or woman. So even if your boss isn't great to work for, remind yourself that you are accountable to Jesus. No matter who has the position above yours, your Lord is always in charge of your future.

PRAYER

It's all for You, Lord. Every ounce of blood, sweat, and tears. Every effort. Every project. Every relationship struggle. Every financial offering. Every kind word to a stranger. Every "I wish I didn't have to get out of bed, but I guess I'd better." It's all for You. The work that I accomplish in this life isn't for my own benefit; it's to draw others to You. So I'll keep going even when I don't feel like it. I'll keep giving even when no one seems to notice. And I'll keep on loving others even when they're difficult to love. It's Your way, and Your ways are perfect. Amen.

Day 221

THE WORD OF TRUTH

Do not snatch your word of truth from me,
for your regulations are my only hope.
PSALM 119:43 NLT

Bibles wear and tear. Papers get discarded. Hard drives crash. But memorizing scripture assures us that God's Word will never be lost. His truth will always be at our disposal, any moment of the day or night when we need a word of encouragement, of guidance, of hope. Like a phone call from heaven, our Father communicates to us via scripture implanted in our hearts. But it's up to us to build the signal tower.

PRAYER

Oh, how I love Your Word, Lord. It truly is a lamp to my feet and a light to my path. When I bury those precious words deep in my heart, they are there, ready, when I need them. They come springing up, a lovely reminder that You are always with me. I'm so grateful for the Bible. Your words are our companions, always! Thank You for giving us this precious love letter. It shows us how to live, how to love, and how to find our way to You, our wonderful Savior. Amen.

Day 222

SERIOUS BUSINESS

Make it your ambition to lead a quiet life: You should mind your own business and work with your hands.

1 THESSALONIANS 4:11 NIV

Whether we work at a computer or on a factory production line, those of us who work with our hands shouldn't feel unimportant. Manual labor is serious business in God's sight. Christians who quietly, faithfully go about their business day by day make an important contribution, bearing God's message to a wide range of people. What a testimony our lives become when we live out this verse!

PRAYER

It's so wonderful to have something to contribute, Lord. Baking cookies for an elderly neighbor. Playing games with the grandkids. Working in the nursery at church. Fostering a sick puppy. These are all ways to make a difference. I don't always feel like I'm contributing much, but I'm learning that You see the little things as big things. So I'll keep writing those kind notes to my coworkers. I'll smile at the woman in the grocery store who looks lonely. I'll take meals to those who are sick. And I'll do it all out of great love for You—and them. Amen.

Day 223

BLAMELESS

[Jesus] has brought you into his own presence, and you are holy and blameless as you stand before him without a single fault.

COLOSSIANS 1:22 NLT

Holiness. Wouldn't we all like to attain it? But it's impossible. Even if we shaved our heads, ate only birdseed, renounced makeup, and wore nothing but muumuus, we still wouldn't be holy. (We'd just be unattractive.) The only way we can achieve holiness is through Jesus, who by His death on our behalf ushers us into the presence of God, blameless, beautiful, and whole. And we can leave our muumuus at home.

PRAYER

I'll never be good enough in my own strength, Lord. I know, because I've tried and failed miserably! It's Your righteousness, Your salvation, that covers me now. I'm still doing my best to live a holy life, to do things that please Your heart. But even though I give it my best effort, I still fall short and need to rely on Your grace. Thank You for that grace! Thank You for Your work on the cross that covered every sin, every stain. I can truly walk with my head held high, knowing I'm covered—head to toe—by Your righteousness. Amen.

Day 224

MORE THAN TEMPORARY

Do not be afraid when one becomes rich, when the glory of his house is increased; for when he dies he shall carry nothing away; his glory shall not descend after him.

PSALM 49:16–17 NKJV

This is the Bible's way of saying, "You can't take it with you." When life ends, the only treasures that remain are the works we have done for Jesus. Money and fame cling to earth, soon to be forgotten. So when unbelievers seem to get all the goodies, we just remember that the treasures we send ahead to heaven are greater than any temporary gain.

PRAYER

I know so many people who are working to gain riches, Lord. It's kind of crazy to see how they collect so much stuff. Huge houses. Fancy cars. Expensive jewelry. Not that there's anything wrong with those things, but I'm reminded that none of those items will be traveling with us to heaven. When I pass away, I won't be taking my favorite diamond ring with me. (Hey, I'll have pearly gates to gaze upon!) My house? It won't be going either. (I'll have a mansion in heaven.) Nothing can begin to compare with what I'll experience in eternity with You. Amen.

Day 225

WHOLE AND HEALED

Pray for each other so that you can live together whole and healed. The prayer of a person living right with God is something powerful to be reckoned with.

JAMES 5:16 MSG

Do you have soul siblings? Brothers and sisters in Christ? Caring people who pray for you and with you about, well, everything? Like a life preserver in a turbulent sea, prayer partners are buoyancy for the soul and security through any storm. Heart bonds, once established, create a trusting environment where we can bare our souls before the Lord in mutual prayer to become whole and healed. Prayer partners are warm hugs from God.

PRAYER

I don't know where I would be without my praying friends, Lord. They are the glue that holds me together on rough days and the laughter that buoys me on the fun days! Together, we're a force to be reckoned with! There's something so powerful about the prayers of like-minded believers. They give me courage, hope, peace, joy, and so much more. I honestly don't know how folks manage without prayer-warrior friends. They are worth more than rubies or gold to me. Thanks so much for surrounding me with the best! Amen.

Day 226

BELONG TO JESUS

"If you belonged to the world, it would love you as its own. As it is, you do not belong to the world, but I have chosen you out of the world. That is why the world hates you."

JOHN 15:19 NIV

Don't expect the world to love you for loving Jesus. Because He doesn't accept its evil, and neither do you, the world is at enmity with both of you. That's not such a bad thing. Who would you rather belong to: Jesus, who holds eternity's joys in His hands, or the world, which offers so much sin and pain?

PRAYER

I'm at odds with this world, Jesus, and it's because I'm Your child. You said in Your Word that I wouldn't fit in—that I should be in the world but not of the world. And I've definitely seen that come to pass as I've tried to connect with people who don't know You and don't understand my faith-walk. The world is definitely not my friend. And yet I know You've placed me here for a reason, to make a difference, to draw people to You. So lead me step by step, Lord, that I might be effective for Your kingdom. Amen.

Day 227

SLATHERED IN SPF

You are my refuge and my shield;
I have put my hope in your word.
PSALM 119:114 NIV

These days, the word *shield* evokes images of glistening sunbathers dotting beaches and carefree children slathered in sunscreen. Like the psalmist's metal shield, sunscreen deflects dangerous rays, preventing them from penetrating vulnerable skin—and we use a higher SPF for more protection. By immersing ourselves in God's Word, we erect a shield that deflects Satan's attempts to penetrate our weak flesh. Internalizing more of God's Word creates a higher SPF: Scripture Protection Factor. Are you well coated?

PRAYER

I'm so grateful for Your Word, Lord. I slather it on, like lotion, to protect, guide, and comfort me along life's highway. So many times (and in so many ways) verses and passages from the Bible have spared me pain and kept me from harm. It's truly remarkable how Your Word covers every topic known to man. No matter what I'm going through, there's a verse for me. I know, because I've been through a lot and I've always found scriptures to help. You truly thought of everything, Lord. Thank You for Your Word. Amen.

Day 228

A PRAYERFUL SOLUTION

I want the men everywhere to pray, lifting up holy hands without anger or disputing.
1 TIMOTHY 2:8 NIV

Anger can become a real trap, even for Christians. When we try to settle differences angrily, we land in big trouble that affects and sometimes even destroys a whole congregation. One solution to anger is prayer. It's hard to stay angry with someone you pray for, even if that person continues to irritate you. As God's Spirit works in your heart, you give the other person a second, a third, or even a hundred and third chance. In Jesus, unrighteous anger cannot linger.

PRAYER

I've been caught in the trap of anger on occasion, Lord. It's no fun. Like a wild beast trying to break free, I do my best, but I can't seem to loosen the bonds of that trap on my own. I cry out to You for supernatural rescue, and You come through. You offer peace in place of anger, joy in place of bitterness. I honestly don't know how You pull it off, Father, but You always manage to free me just when I need it. Thank You for releasing me from the trap that once ensnared me. I'm eternally grateful. Amen.

Day 229

THE FOUNDATION AND FINALE

I hope to see you soon, and then we will talk face to face. Peace be with you.

3 JOHN 1:14–15 NLT

My prayer is that the message you receive from this book is that Christ is the ultimate source of hope. We can live without many things, but we cannot live without hope. It's the air we breathe, the water that invigorates every molecule of our being, the motivation that drives us. Hope enriches and empowers us, connecting us with our Papa God. Hope is the essence of our faith. It's the foundation and the finale.

PRAYER

Hope is the thread that holds so many things in my life together, Lord. I've been hopeless a time or two, and I remember how all the different areas of my life fell apart. When I put my hope in You, everything works out better. Much better. When I take my eyes off You? Well, things disintegrate. Hope gives me courage to go on. Hope lifts my spirits. Hope puts air in my lungs. And You, Lord? You're the source of my hope. If not for You, I would truly have nothing. Thank You for empowering me with hope for the situations I face today. Amen.

Day 230

LETTING GO OF ANGER

Now the works of the flesh are evident,
which are: adultery, . . .idolatry, sorcery, hatred,
contentions, jealousies, outbursts of wrath.
GALATIANS 5:19–20 NKJV

It's not something we like to hear, but according to God, anger is right up there with sins such as adultery and idolatry.

Most of us feel wrathful occasionally. But if such feelings take hold of our lives and bitterness results, we fall into sin. When anger touches our reactions, let's heed it as a warning sign of an issue that requires our attention. Through wise action and prayer, we can let go of anger and trust the Lord to replace it with His peace.

PRAYER

I'll admit it, Lord. . .I sometimes let my anger get the best of me. It usually catches me off guard, surprising everyone in the room, myself included. Often it's reactionary. I kick back at an injustice or a perceived threat. But afterward I'm typically filled with regret. I feel bad for lashing out (sometimes at folks who were completely innocent). Thank You for the reminder that I can't let anger control me. It's not my puppeteer. You can calm my heart and show me a better way. May I never let anger be my ruler. Amen.

Day 231

SHOUTS OF JOY

"He will yet fill your mouth with laughter and your lips with shouts of joy."

JOB 8:21 NIV

Do you remember the last time you laughed till you cried? For many of us, it has been far too long. Stress tends to steal our joy, leaving us humorless and oh-so-serious. But lightness and fun haven't disappeared forever. They may be buried beneath the snow of a long, wintry life season, but spring is coming, girls. Laughter will bloom again, and our hearts will soar as our lips shout with joy. Grasp that hope!

PRAYER

Oh, how I love the release that laughter brings, Lord! It changes everything. A good belly laugh can lift my mood, change my attitude, and release endorphins to begin the healing process in my body. No wonder Your Word says laughter is good like medicine! In some ways it's better because it's free, it's easy to come by, and it doesn't require a prescription! Thank You for always giving us something to laugh about, even when times are tough. Keeping a good sense of humor is key to walking out a joy-filled life! Amen.

Day 232

TODAY!

"Therefore do not worry about tomorrow, for tomorrow will worry about itself. Each day has enough trouble of its own."

MATTHEW 6:34 NIV

You can look ahead and obsess over fears for the future, or you can take life one day at a time and enjoy it. But you only live in today, not in the weeks, months, and years that may lie ahead. Since worry never improves the future and only hurts today, you'll benefit most from trusting in God and enjoying the spot where He has planted you for now.

PRAYER

I'm so glad You've encouraged us to live one day at a time, Lord. I get anxious when I think about the future. There's a lot to worry about if one is prone to worry. And You know me, Lord. Sometimes I fret about what's up ahead. So I'll do my best to stay focused on today. It's a gift, meant to be lived to the fullest. I'll lose track of my joy if I look past the gift that's in front of me only to focus on the what-ifs of my tomorrows. You have it all handled anyway. (Have I mentioned how grateful I am for that?) Thank You, Lord! Amen.

Day 233

I'M NO EEYORE

Then [Job's] wife said to him, "Do you still hold firm your integrity? Curse God and die!"

Job 2:9 NASB

Job's wife was the unwilling recipient of Satan's attacks because of her husband's righteous life. When the going got tough, our girl lost faith and her hope disintegrated. We too sometimes lose sight of all God has done for us and focus only on what He hasn't done. Our optimistic attitudes are consumed by negativity. Job's response is the key to escaping the shackles of Eeyore-ism: "I know that my Redeemer lives" (Job 19:25 NASB).

PRAYER

I don't want to be a complainer, Lord. I don't want people to flinch when I come around or to say things like, "Oh, great. It's her." I'll admit, I whine a bit. Okay, sometimes a lot. But help me direct those complaints to You and not to others. Whining and complaining suck the joy out of a room in a hurry! Instead of being known for my grievances and grumbling, let me be known for my joy, Lord! When I enter the room, let every face light up as people say, "Oh, good! She's here! We needed a ray of sunshine today!" Amen.

Day 234

SHARING WITH JESUS

Casting all your care upon him; for he careth for you.

1 PETER 5:7 KJV

You don't have a care in the world that you cannot share—with Jesus, that is. There isn't one thing He doesn't want to hear about from you. Before you ask a friend to pray for you (and you should do that), be certain you share your care with your best friend, Jesus. Your human friend may try to help you and may do a lot for you, but no one helps like Jesus. There's no worry He can't alleviate or remove.

PRAYER

I'm grateful for the friends You've placed in my life, Father. They mean the world to me. They listen. They care. They try to help. But no one—absolutely no one—hears me like You do. Oh, they hear me with their physical ears, but they don't always hear the true cries of my heart. I'm so glad You listen for the heart behind the words. And I'm also grateful for Your caring, loving responses when I hit rock bottom. You crawl down into the depths just to wrap Your arms around me. Thank You, Father! Amen.

Day 235

CONFOUNDED CORSETS

Cultivate inner beauty, the gentle, gracious kind that God delights in.

1 PETER 3:4 MSG

In our quest for beauty, we buy into all sorts of crazy things: mud facials, cosmetic surgery, body piercings, obsessive dieting, squeezing size 10 feet into size 8 shoes. The image of Scarlett O'Hara's binding corset makes us shudder. (Reminds me of a pair of jeans I wrestled with just last week.) Yet God's idea of beauty is on the inside—where spandex cannot touch. Let's resolve to devote more time to pursuing inner beauty that will never require Botox.

PRAYER

I'm so glad You're more interested in the inside than the outside, Lord. I've done everything I can to make the outside look its level best, but I'm still no beauty queen. Not by the world's standards, anyway. You, though? You're looking at my heart. As long as I keep it clean and pure, You see it as a thing of beauty. And because I'm created in Your image—I'm Your child—You view me as beautiful too. Thanks for reminding me that I'm loved and seen and adored by the King of the world! Amen.

Day 236

POWERFUL PRAYER

"The Lord bless you and keep you; the Lord make his face shine on you and be gracious to you."
Numbers 6:24–25 NIV

Want to pray for someone? This is a good way to do it. It's the blessing God gave to Aaron and his sons to pronounce on Israel. What Christian wouldn't appreciate these words, committing her to God's care and wanting her to draw closer to Him? Who would turn down the good things God has to offer? Can you bless your friends and family with these thoughts today?

PRAYER

One of the greatest joys of my life, Lord, is that You've instructed me to pray for others. It's not just a gift I give that person; it's a gift to me as well. When I pray for someone I love—or even an enemy—it's a reminder of how much You love them. It shifts my focus off myself and onto someone else. And I know that's how You've called me to live. Today I pray Aaron's blessing on my friends, my family, and even those who haven't been so kind to me. Bless them, Lord. Truly. Amen.

Day 237

GOOD ENOUGH

Leah's eyes were weak, but Rachel was beautiful in figure and appearance.
GENESIS 29:17 NASB

Have you ever felt like a booby prize? No doubt Leah did. Hunky Jacob labored seven years to marry Leah's gorgeous sister, Rachel. Then their squirrelly father switched his daughters at the altar. Jacob freaked. Leah tanked. We too sometimes feel that we're not good enough—that we don't measure up. But Leah gave birth to six of the twelve tribes of Israel, the cornerstone of Judeo-Christendom. God has a mighty plan for all of us Leahs.

PRAYER

I'm so glad I don't have to measure up, Lord. If I fall short—physically, emotionally, or even in my talents and abilities—You pick up the slack. (Whew!) I don't have to be good enough. You love me and use me regardless. When I think of how You used Leah to give birth to six of the twelve tribes of Israel, it's easy to see that You have much bigger plans than I can see with my own eyes. I don't know what You're going to do in and through me, but I'm here to say, "I'm ready!" Use me, Lord. Amen.

Day 238

LIVING FOR CHRIST

If you live according to the flesh, you will die; but if by the Spirit you put to death the misdeeds of the body, you will live.

ROMANS 8:13 NIV

Living for Christ through His Spirit is real life, abundant and overflowing. Blessings spill over in obedient lives. But the world, at war with God, doesn't understand. Unbelievers don't feel the touch of the Spirit in their hearts and lives, and Jesus' gentle love is foreign to them. Put to death worldly misdeeds, and instead of the emptiness of the world, you'll receive blessings indeed.

PRAYER

I don't ever want to be at war with You, Lord. Being at odds with my Maker is awkward, uncomfortable, and just plain dangerous! Instead, I want to live fully for You each day, led by Your Spirit—hearing Your voice, walking out Your plan, doing Your will. You have great blessings and adventures ahead for me, and I don't want to miss a thing due to my own stubbornness and selfishness. So I will bury those things and rise to live with You. Thanks for the reminder that life is about more than me, myself, and I. Amen.

Day 239

A LITTLE GOES A LONG WAY

"The Lord our God has allowed a few of us to survive as a remnant."
Ezra 9:8 NLT

Remnants. Useless by most standards, but God is in the business of using tiny slivers of what's left to do mighty things. Nehemiah rebuilt the fallen walls of Jerusalem with a remnant of Israel; Noah's three sons repopulated the earth after the flood; four slave boys—Daniel, Shadrach, Meshach, and Abednego—kept faith alive for an entire nation. When it feels as if bits and pieces are all that has survived of your hope, remember how much God can accomplish with remnants!

PRAYER

I don't mind being a remnant, Lord. With You there are no discards, only people of possibility! So even when I'm feeling useless—which happens from time to time—I'm grateful for the reminder that You have big plans for Your kids, even those of us who struggle with insecurity and rejection. It's helpful to remember that the "characters" in the Bible weren't really characters at all. They were very real people who did very real things for You and Your kingdom. May I be just as effective! Amen.

Day 240

AN OBEDIENT LIFE

Blessed are those whose way is blameless,
who walk in the Law of the Lord.
Psalm 119:1 NASB

Want to be blessed? Then don't live a sin-filled life. God can't pour out blessings on anyone who consistently ignores His commands. Blessings belong to those who hear God's Word and take it to heart, living it out in love. Want to be blessed? Obey the Master. You'll live blamelessly and joyfully.

PRAYER

I want to be a vessel You can pour Your blessings into, Lord. But sometimes I'm the one stopping the flow. My actions—or lack thereof—separate me from You. Today I want to acknowledge that and turn from any sins in my life so I can walk in a healthy relationship with You. I'll listen. I'll obey. I'll do all I can to please Your heart, because I know how much You love me. Obeying isn't always easy, but the benefits are out of this world. (Literally!) Thanks for the reminder, Lord. Amen.

Day 241

THE SAM CREED

"If we are thrown into the blazing furnace, the God whom we serve is able to save us. . . . But even if he doesn't, . . .we will never serve your gods."

DANIEL 3:17–18 NLT

Shadrach, Abednego, and Meshach were young Israelite men who were captured and transported as slaves to Babylon. Ordered by their new king to worship his god or die horribly in a fiery furnace, the three young men evoked the SAM Creed, an acronym for their names: My God is able to deliver me, but even if He chooses not to, I will still follow Him. Through tough times, let's resolve to live by the SAM Creed.

PRAYER

I definitely want to learn to live by the SAM Creed, Lord. When I encounter a fiery furnace type of situation in my walk with You, may I face it with as much courage and faith as Shadrach, Abednego, and Meshach did. What a wonderful example they set as they bravely faced potential death. Like those great men of old, may I always say, "You are able, Lord. . .but even if You choose not to deliver me, I will still follow You!" May I trust You always, even in the fiery furnaces of life. Thank You for growing my faith. Amen.

Day 242

SEE YA, SELF

"Blessed are the poor in spirit,
for theirs is the kingdom of heaven."
MATTHEW 5:3 NASB

We don't often think of ourselves as "poor in spirit," but this passage refers to those who are not full of themselves—those who are filled instead with God's Spirit. "Poor" in this context means selfless rather than selfish; it refers to those with an attitude of dependence on God. How do we become poor in spirit and revel in the hope and promise of heaven? By emptying ourselves of self and the pride of self-sufficiency and refilling ourselves with Jesus.

PRAYER

Emptying myself of pride isn't easy, Lord. I've learned this the hard way. I tend to run on the selfish side at times. I guess we all do. But You want me to be poor in spirit—to pull the plug on self and refill myself with You. That's my choice today! Fill me up. Squeeze out every drop of selfishness and flood me with Your power and might and the strength to carry out Your perfect will for my life. I long for Your Spirit to rule and reign, to be my guide and my decision-making strategy. May I always be dependent on You and never myself. Amen.

Day 243

THE GIFT OF CHILDREN

Children are a heritage from the Lord,
offspring a reward from him.
Psalm 127:3 NIV

Today, many people see children more as a punishment than a reward. But when you hear of parents who wish they had never had children, you know they're missing out. God creates families to love each other and share His joys. Parents who honestly live out their faith in front of their children can guide them into enjoying a good family life with their own kids someday, and the cycle can continue. Are your children a blessing? He has given them to You as a reward, not as a punishment. Do you treat them that way?

PRAYER

Thank You for rewarding us with kiddos, Lord! Whether they're my own or a friend's or grandkids, children are a blessing I don't want to miss. I love their smiling faces, their rippling laughter, and the way they view the world through eyes of imagination. I'm crazy about their little freckled faces, messy hair, and mismatched shoes. No matter what they look like (or how they act), children are our heritage, our reward, our blessing. May I set a good example in the way I treat them, Lord, so that others will learn to love them as I do. Amen.

Day 244

CAT-I-TUDE VERSUS DOG-I-TUDE

Lord, the LORD Almighty, may those who hope in you not be disgraced because of me.

PSALM 69:6 NIV

Are you a hisser or a wagger?

Perhaps you have a feline attitude: It's all about me. I like you for what you can do for me. You'll have my attention only when it's convenient for me. Me, me, me.

Or maybe you have a dog mentality: It's all about you. I love you unconditionally just because you're you. How can I make you happy? God is glorified by selflessness, not selfishness. Let's strive to make our Master proud.

PRAYER

I don't want to be a whiner and hisser, Lord. I don't want to be so focused on my own stuff that I miss out on blessing others. Make me more like Fido when it comes to my attitude and the way I treat others. Help me to be outward focused, caring about the people You've placed around me. I want to be known as someone who loves unconditionally, not as one who is always whining and complaining. This will take work, I know. Please help me take my eyes off myself and live as You would have me live. Amen.

Day 245

WISE CORRECTION

A rod and a reprimand impart wisdom,
but a child left undisciplined disgraces its mother.
PROVERBS 29:15 NIV

In today's world, fears of child abuse have caused us to ignore this verse. Have we therefore missed the power of correction, which gives our children wisdom? As God restrains us from wrongdoing, we need to stop our children too. We need not touch a child physically to modify behavior. Will we discipline harmful actions now or lose the chance to be proud of our self-controlled children who love the Lord?

PRAYER

We all need a little behavior modification from time to time, Lord. I know I do! *Discipline* isn't a bad word, as long as it's carried out in a loving, biblical manner. When I think of how lovingly You've disciplined me over the years—when I remember how You somehow managed to correct and chasten me while still wrapping Your arms around me—I know it's possible. May I learn from the beautiful example You have set. May I discipline with that same degree of love and affection. Guide me, I pray. Amen.

Day 246

COMFORTING THE COMFORTLESS

He brings us alongside someone else who is going through hard times so that we can be there for that person just as God was there for us.

2 CORINTHIANS 1:4 MSG

Heartbroken and hollow after my sixth miscarriage, I struggled to find meaning in my loss. My heavenly Father's arms comforted me when I burst into tears at song lyrics or at the sight of a mother cuddling her infant in Walmart. I finally relinquished my babies to Jesus' loving embrace, confident that I'd see them again one day. I was then able to share His comfort and hope with other women suffering miscarriages.

PRAYER

Grief can be so heavy, so overpowering, Lord. I've been swallowed up in it far too many times to count. How I've depended on Your comfort during those difficult times! Now You're showing me that I can take this road I've walked, with all of its disappointments and pain, and somehow use it to minister to others who are hurting. I know it won't be easy, but please use me as You see fit, Father, to bring comfort and hope to those who are at the end of their rope right now. I want to bring hope and healing. Amen.

Day 247

RUN INTO HIS ARMS

Just as we share abundantly in the sufferings of Christ, so also our comfort abounds through Christ.
2 CORINTHIANS 1:5 NIV

Paul knew the pain of persecution, but he also knew the deep comfort God offered. When people gave the apostle trouble, God drew His servant close to His heart. When trials come your way, God will do the same for you. If life is always going smoothly, comfort is meaningless; but when you're in the midst of trouble, He comes alongside with tender love that supersedes your trials and reaches out to others.

PRAYER

Sometimes I just have to pull away, Lord—from the crowd, the chaos, the opinions, the pain. I need You-and-me time. When I'm hurting, when my heart is broken, I find healing in Your presence as I sense Your arms around me. But I struggle to connect with You when I'm surrounded on every side. So today I come running into Your arms. Those things that are troubling me? I'll give them to You. That pain in my heart? It's Yours too. Thank You for flooding my soul with peace in spite of the pain! Amen.

Day 248

LOOSE LIPS

We all make many mistakes. For if we could control our tongues, we would be perfect and could also control ourselves in every other way.

JAMES 3:2 NLT

Many of us don't let thoughts marinate long before we spew them out of our mouths. We want to honor God with our speech but seem to spend more time dousing forest fires resulting from sparks kindled by our wagging tongues (James 3:5). Don't despair! There's hope for loose lips! The Creator of self-control is happy to loan us a muzzle (Psalm 39:1) if we sincerely want to change.

PRAYER

How often I've been guilty of speaking without thinking, Lord! I open my mouth and words just fly out. Oh, how I wish I could take them back. But usually it's too late. I should look into purchasing a muzzle, perhaps. Help me to guard my words, Lord. May Your Spirit "muzzle" me as needed before unhelpful words escape. And please guard my heart too; I know that the words spewing from my mouth are triggered by what's going on in my heart. I want to honor You, Lord, in all I say and do. Amen.

Day 249

TENDER COMFORT

"As one whom his mother comforts, so I will comfort you."
ISAIAH 66:13 NKJV

Like a tender mother, God comforts His people. When life challenges us, we can turn to the Lord to renew our faith. Instead of questioning God's compassion because we face a trial, we can draw ever nearer to Him, seeking to do His will. Surrounded by His tender arms, we gain strength to go out and face the world again.

PRAYER

I sometimes wonder how You can be so tender with us, Lord. We aren't always so good to You. Most parents would knee-jerk and react to their naughty kids, but You? You always have such a way of drawing us close, whispering words of love and forgiveness, then showing us a better way. That tenderness is inspiring. It makes me want to be more like You—not just with the children in my life but with friends, coworkers, and even my spouse. Show me how to love like You love. Show me how to comfort like You comfort. I want to be more like You, Jesus. Amen.

Day 250

THE EYES HAVE IT

All of you together are Christ's body,
and each of you is a part of it.
1 CORINTHIANS 12:27 NLT

Just as our bodies are made up of many parts, each essential for functioning as a whole, the body of Christ is made up of hands, feet, ears, hearts, and minds. We women understand this concept but tend to compare ourselves to others. If we're hands, we wish we were feet. If we're noses, we'd rather be eyes. Sometimes we feel like bunions. But God views us as equally important, none better than another. Even us toenails!

PRAYER

Thanks for seeing us all as equally important, Lord. There have been times when I felt like a freckle on the nose of the church and nothing more. Just a little blemish people have to contend with. But I know that's not true. I'm a voice for You. I am the hands and feet of Christ, carrying the gospel message to others. You are able to use every part of me to minister to this world as various needs arise. So thank You for guarding my heart. I don't want to get caught up in the comparison game, wishing I was like those around me. I'm okay being me. Amen.

Day 251

GIVER OF COMFORT

You ought to forgive and comfort him, so that he will not be overwhelmed by excessive sorrow.

2 CORINTHIANS 2:7 NIV

Do you know someone who is sorry for her sin? Then don't keep reminding her of it. If she has sought forgiveness and put it behind her, it's dead. Instead of criticizing, remind her of the power of God that works in her life. Encourage her when temptation calls her name. Then she won't be overcome by sorrow and fall into sin again. Give comfort, and you will be a blessing.

PRAYER

I've been in that place so many times, Lord, where I've asked for forgiveness but can't seem to forgive myself. It's even harder to let go of my sin when people keep reminding me of it. "Hey, remember that time you. . ." Those moments are like a knife in the heart. I'd rather move on, and with Your help I can. Keep me focused on You and Your Word. May I never forget that You've already forgiven me—You pardoned me the moment I asked. There's no point in beating myself up over something You've long since forgotten! Amen.

Day 252

HOLDING HANDS

When I am afraid, I will put my trust in You.
PSALM 56:3 NASB

While I cowered in a bathroom stall before my first speaking event, my queasy stomach rolled and sweat beaded on my forehead. I prayed for a way to escape. Into my head popped a childhood memory verse: "When I am afraid, I will put my trust in You." My pounding heart calmed. I repeated the scripture aloud and felt my nausea subside and panic diminish. Peace flooded my soul.

When we're afraid, Papa God is right beside us holding our hand.

PRAYER

I know what it's like to cower in fear, Lord. I've been doubled over many times. Fear grips and I'm frozen in place, unable to perform the tasks in front of me, even the simplest ones. Then You whisper words of comfort and solace. You remind me that I can put my trust in You, even if my feelings are crying out otherwise. So I take a deep breath and do my best to allow Your Spirit to console and redirect me. Thank You for the reminder that I don't have to live in fear, Lord. I can truly be set free with Your help. Amen.

Day 253

GOD'S PROVISION

Now godliness with contentment is great gain.
1 TIMOTHY 6:6 NKJV

Paul warned Timothy against false teachers who wanted to use the church for financial gain. If these people were looking for security, they were on the wrong track. Money, which comes and goes, never brings real protection. Our security lies in God's provision. No matter the size of our bank account, we can feel content in Jesus. The one who brought us into this world will never forget that we require food, clothing, and all the rest. When we truly trust in Jesus, contentment is sure to follow.

PRAYER

I'm so glad my provision isn't up to me, Lord. I don't have the capability to come up with all I need. But You do! You own the cattle on a thousand hills. You also know exactly what I need and when I need it. So when I'm panicked, wondering where the next bit of provision is going to come from, You're already on the job, working to supply what I need. I can't see it until it arrives, but I choose to put my faith in You no matter what. (And boy, Your timing is excellent!) Thanks for supplying my every need. Amen.

Day 254

DOWN WITH FLAB

Workouts in the gymnasium are useful, but a disciplined life in God is far more so, making you fit both today and forever.

1 TIMOTHY 4:7–8 MSG

Do you have Dumbo flaps? You know, those fleshy wings that hang from the undersides of your arms when you raise them? A stiff wind could create liftoff. They say regular workouts will tighten those puppies up. . .and significantly reduce wind shear. Just as we exercise muscles to make them strong, we keep our faith in shape by exercising it. Discipline is the way to conquer flab—physically and spiritually!

PRAYER

Sometimes I forget to exercise my faith, Lord. It gets flabby. I lean on my own understanding, my own way of doing things. I forget that You are already at work behind the scenes. Weeks go by. Months, even. And I wonder why I feel so weak, so helpless. Then I realize my faith has completely atrophied. Today I choose to turn that around. I once again take my hands off the situations in front of me and place them back into Your capable hands. I acknowledge that You're in control. . .and I trust You. Amen.

Day 255

CONTENTMENT IN TROUBLE

The fear of the LORD *leads to life;*
then one rests content, untouched by trouble.
PROVERBS 19:23 NIV

God doesn't promise we will never suffer trouble, but He does promise something even more important. In the middle of trouble, we will experience real life—contentment in the middle of confusion, doubt, or turmoil. Which would you prefer: trouble and life in Jesus, or trouble on its own? You can't avoid trouble here on earth. But share life with Him, and contentment will follow.

PRAYER

I'm learning to be content in every situation, Lord. Emphasis on the word *learning*. Contentment doesn't come naturally to me. But my mindset is different now. Instead of whining and complaining about my circumstances, I'm learning to express gratitude, even when I'm unhappy. "Thank You for this ten-year-old car with the cracked windshield. It's getting me where I need to go." The truth is, You cover all my needs. And my wants? Well, they might come in time. But even if they don't, I'll do my best to be content with what I have. Amen.

Day 256

BIGGER THAN FEAR

Having hope will give you courage.
You will be protected and will rest in safety.
JOB 11:18 NLT

Tossing, turning, sleepless nights—what woman doesn't know these intimately? Our thoughts race with what-ifs and fear steals our peace. How precious then is God's promise that He will rescue us from nagging, faceless fear and give us courage to just say no to anxious thoughts that threaten to terrorize us in our most vulnerable moments. He is our hope and protector. He is bigger than fear. Anxiety flees in His presence. Rest in Him tonight.

PRAYER

I want to rest in You, Lord, but it's not always easy. In spite of my best attempts to let go of my problems, many times they linger in my thoughts and in my heart. I want to shake them but they live on, often keeping me awake at night. I toss and turn, wondering how I can fix things, when in reality these situations were never mine to fix. Please give me the courage to say no to anxiety. Help me realize it's not my friend. You will always be my hope and protector, so I will keep my eyes on You, not myself. Amen.

Day 257

ETERNAL PERSPECTIVE

"Where, O death, is your victory?
Where, O death, is your sting?"
1 CORINTHIANS 15:55 NIV

Nothing in this world diminishes the pain of death. The grief of losing one we love reaches deep into our souls. But through His sacrifice, Jesus permanently overcame the sting of mortality. Those who trust in Him don't live for a few short years but for eternity. When their earthly life ends, they simply move into heaven.

When we lose loved ones, our hearts feel pain. But if they gave their lives to Jesus, He is still victorious. In time we will meet them again in paradise.

PRAYER

Oh Lord, how it hurts to lose someone I love! It feels like an out-of-body experience, like it's not really happening. How can it be that someone I knew and loved so deeply no longer exists? And yet she does exist! She lives on with You, a fact that gives me hope and comfort. She also lives on in me, through my experiences and memories. You, Jesus, overcame the sting of death, and You are the only one who can bring comfort when I need it most. Thank You for the reminder that grief will give way to victory! Amen.

Day 258

SMILING IN THE DARKNESS

The hopes of the godless evaporate.

Job 8:13 NLT

Hope isn't just an emotion; it's a perspective, a discipline, a way of life. It's a journey of choice. We must learn to override those messages of discouragement, despair, and fear that assault us in times of trouble and press toward the light. Hope is smiling in the darkness. It's confidence that faith in God's sovereignty amounts to something. . .something life-changing, lifesaving, and eternal.

PRAYER

Hope really is smiling in the darkness, Lord. And that's when I need it most. The darkness encompasses me and makes me feel completely hopeless. It's hard to see beyond the shadows. But hope brings light—little flickering shimmers of light—to my pathway. And once I can adjust my eyes, my heart perks up. I start to feel more confident. Thank You for shining light onto my hopelessness and giving me a reason to keep going. I place my trust, my faith, in You today, Lord! Amen.

Day 259

DEATH WILL DIE

The last enemy to be destroyed is death.
1 CORINTHIANS 15:26 NIV

If Jesus conquered death, why do we still suffer the death of loved ones? Because today we live in the promise of death's destruction, not its completion. God's Son has ransomed us through His sacrifice, but death still exists in our world. One day, that will no longer be so. Jesus promises to destroy death entirely—death shall die, and heaven will be ours.

PRAYER

You never wanted Your children to have to face death, did You, Lord? As I read through the book of Genesis, it's easy to see that You always had a plan for us to walk out whole, healthy lives in Your presence, apart from sickness, pain, and death. But mankind blew it, and death entered the picture as a result of sin. Now we all—at some point—must cross the threshold from this life to the next. For believers, You've made that process so much easier with the promise of heaven. May more and more people come to know You so that they can live forever with You! Amen.

Day 260

LET ME BE

"Martha, . . .you are worried and upset about many things, but few things are needed—or indeed only one. Mary has chosen what is better."

LUKE 10:41–42 NIV

Martha zipped around cleaning, cooking, and organizing. Meanwhile, Mary sat at Jesus' feet. Many of us think like Martha. Will food magically appear on the table? Will the house clean itself? We're slaves to endless to-do lists. Our need to do overwhelms our desire to be. Constipated calendars attest that we are human doings instead of human beings. But Jesus taught that Mary chose best: simply to be. Lord, help this doer learn to be.

PRAYER

I'm such a doer, Lord. You gave me an innate desire to get things done, and I love it! But there are times, I must confess, that I'm more of a "doer" than a "be-er." You want me to just be. To sit at Your feet. To enjoy my downtime. To rest. To refresh. But that's hard when I'm buzzing around taking care of things. Thank You for the reminder that quiet time with You is critical—to my spiritual health and my physical health. I want to draw near and be with You so that I can grow in my faith and in my walk with You, my Savior. Amen.

Day 261

BE FAITHFUL

Good and upright is the Lord;
therefore he instructs sinners in his ways.
Psalm 25:8 NIV

Don't know which way to turn or where to go? God will show you. Just be faithful to Him and you will hear His still, small voice guiding you—or you also may find that circumstances and wise advisers are illuminating the path you need to walk on.

Still doubting? Ask God for forgiveness for sins that bar your communion with Him. Soon, with a clean heart, you'll be headed in the right direction.

PRAYER

Sometimes I feel turned around. Discombobulated. Lost. I honestly can't find my internal compass. Then I remember You're right beside me, Lord. I reach to take Your hand. I ask for Your help. And You begin to guide me, step by step, to where I need to go. I never have to give in to that lost feeling again, because You've promised to always be my guide. You gave me Your Holy Spirit as an internal compass so that I would always know which way to go. Thank You for those Spirit-nudges when I get off course! Amen.

Day 262

DWELLING PLACE

Do you not know that you are a temple of God and that the Spirit of God dwells in you?
1 CORINTHIANS 3:16 NASB

Have you ever been awed by the beauty of a majestic cathedral with towering ceilings inlaid with gold and silver, magnificent paintings, rich carpets, and stained-glass windows? Only the finest for the house of God Almighty.

Did you know God thinks of you and me as living cathedrals—dwelling places of His Spirit? How amazing to be considered worthy of such an honor! How immeasurable His love to choose us as His dwelling place!

PRAYER

What a lovely reminder of how You see me, Lord! You view me as a gorgeous cathedral ready to be filled with praises to You. Today I ask You to make me a sanctuary. Fill every nook and cranny of me with Your presence. I offer You all of me—even the parts I see as broken and flawed. You breathe new life into those places and turn them into stained-glass windows, chandeliers, and altars. I am a temple of Your Spirit. You are my God. Thank You for choosing to dwell inside of me, Lord. Amen.

Day 263

MOVING MOUNTAINS

"Whoever says to this mountain, 'Be removed and be cast into the sea,' and does not doubt. . . but believes. . .will have whatever he says."
MARK 11:23 NKJV

Don't you wish you had faith like this? Christians often try to gear up to it, willing it with all their hearts. But that's not what God had in mind. Manipulating Him cannot work.

Only when we fully trust in Him will He move our mountain—even if it's in an unexpected direction.

PRAYER

Sometimes I read this verse and I'm disappointed that my faith hasn't been so strong, Lord. I haven't seen mountains move. Then I remember that I probably have seen mountains move and just didn't realize it at the time. Like when my friend was near death and we prayed. . .and You performed the miraculous. Or when my marriage was in trouble and You somehow healed the rift. You've done miraculous things right in front of me. Those proverbial mountains seemed impossible to navigate. . .but then You stepped in. Thank You, my mountain-moving God! Amen.

Day 264

BRICK BY BRICK

So then faith cometh by hearing,
and hearing by the word of God.
ROMANS 10:17 KJV

Words are powerful. They cut. They heal. They confirm. God uses His Word to help us, to challenge us, to mold us, to make us more like Him. Our faith is built from the bricks of God's Word. Brick by brick, we build and strengthen and fortify that faith. But only if we truly listen and hear the Word of God.

PRAYER

The longer I walk with You and the deeper I delve into Your Word, the stronger I get, Lord. I really am growing, brick by brick. On those days when I'm not feeling it (and there are plenty of them), remind me of the progress that has already been made. I'm not who I used to be. I'm growing in You. Then show me how to mentor others so that they can grow too. Take me deep into Your Word, learning its nuances, so that I can apply it to my life and make lasting changes—in my own life and in the lives of others. Amen.

Day 265

BE PREPARED

He has also set eternity in the human heart; yet no one can fathom what God has done from beginning to end.

ECCLESIASTES 3:11 NIV

Though each of us has a bit of eternity in our hearts and we cannot rest unless we know the Savior, we also cannot fathom the works of God. Either that truth can make us dissatisfied and doubtful, or it can lead us to become relaxed, trusting children who know that their Father is in control and will care for them from beginning to end. Have you trusted Him who is the Alpha and Omega? Are you prepared for eternity with Him?

PRAYER

There's something inside of me that always longed for You, Lord. You were the missing piece to the puzzle that I didn't even know existed. And when that piece slipped into place, everything made sense. Suddenly I understood why my heart always yearned for heaven. You are in control of my days—from the moment of my conception all the way through to eternity. There's no end date now that I'm walking with You. And how amazing to realize that You always knew I would spend eternity with You, even before I was conceived! Amen.

Day 266

ENDURING WITH GRACE

Endurance builds character, which gives us
a hope that will never disappoint us.
ROMANS 5:4–5 CEV

Heroes come in all kinds of packages. My eighteen-year-old niece, Andie, has cerebral palsy and is legally blind. It takes her four times longer than the average person to do just about anything. But she does it anyway—playing drums, walking in leg braces, attending college. Some days, the frustration of being different overwhelms her. But through endurance, she has developed inspiring character traits: rock-solid faith, contagious hope, and a stellar sense of humor. When I grow up, I want to be like Andie.

PRAYER

Enduring is not a word I enjoy, Lord. I would rather sail through life without any complications than have to endure the hard stuff. Sometimes I'm guilty of whining and complaining about how hard I have it. Then I see the struggles others are going through and I zip my lips, ready to admit that things really aren't so bad for me. Thank You for the reminder that it's possible to endure with grace. When people speak of me, I hope they say, "She went through some tough stuff, but we rarely heard her complain." Amen.

Day 267

THE CHRISTIAN LIFE

Clearly no one who relies on the law is justified before God, because "the righteous will live by faith."

GALATIANS 3:11 NIV

Though some might claim it, crossing all your t's and dotting all your i's spiritually does not make you a great Christian. Rules and regulations aren't what the Christian life is about. Faith is. Obeying God and following Him as the Spirit leads challenges you to trust Him every moment of your life. With that kind of faith in action, you'll be sharing His world-changing message with everyone around you.

PRAYER

Following the rules is important to many of us, Lord. And I'll admit, I've even used that method in my relationship with You. There were times when I felt that doing the right thing—following all of the biblical commandments—would earn me brownie points with You. But You don't work like that. You know my flaws. You see how far from perfection I am no matter how hard I try. And yet You love me anyway. Thanks for the reminder that the Christian life is really all about faith. I want to put my faith into action to be effective for You! Amen.

Day 268

SMALL BUT MIGHTY

He has. . .exalted the humble.

LUKE 1:52 NLT

God delights in making small things great. He's in the business of taking scrap-heap people and turning them into treasures: Noah (laughingstock of his city), Moses (stuttering shepherd turned national leader), David (smallest among the big and powerful), Sarah (old and childless), Mary (poor teenager), Rahab (harlot turned faith-filled ancestor of Jesus). So you and I can rejoice with hope! Let us glory in our smallness!

PRAYER

Whew! I'm so glad you use everyone, Lord, even those of us who are woefully underqualified! You definitely turn us all into treasures. And more than that, You make us effective for Your kingdom, able to draw people to You by the word of our testimony. (And I'm so grateful for the testimony of what You have done in my life.) I feel such great joy knowing that You exalt me not so I can win applause but so others can be drawn into a relationship with You and ultimately spend eternity with the King of kings! Amen.

Day 269

OUR HEARTS

Are you willing to acknowledge, you foolish person, that faith without works is useless?

JAMES 2:20 NASB

Faith isn't faith if actions don't follow belief. No matter what someone says, unless compassion, love, and kindness accompany her words, it would be foolish to consider her Christian testimony believable.

Though works don't save us, they show what's in our hearts. What are we proving by our works today?

PRAYER

I've heard it all my life, Lord: "Faith without works is dead." There's no point in exhibiting great faith if I'm not able to follow it up with kindness, gentleness, and self-control. I don't just want people to "think" my Christian testimony is believable; I want them to know it! And this means it must be. So please give me faith, but also give me the willingness to go out and actually do the things You're calling me to do. May my outward testimony be a true reflection of what's going on inside my heart, Lord. Amen.

Day 270

I'VE GOT A NAME

"I have redeemed you; I have called you by your name; you are Mine."
ISAIAH 43:1 NKJV

Parents have the indescribable privilege of bestowing a name on their newborn, the identity that little person will be known by for the rest of his or her life. In effect, we give them a part of us. They are an extension of ourselves—our flesh, our blood.

Your heavenly Father has called you by name. He has given you part of Himself: Jesus. You are special to Him. You are His daughter. In this connection, find security. . .comfort. . .hope.

PRAYER

You call me by name, Lord. You know me intimately. Before I was born, You knew who I would be, what I would do, where I would live, and all of the many things I would accomplish. You call me Your child, Your daughter. I am Yours and You are mine. Truly, my relationship with You is the greatest relationship of my life—I'm deeply honored to be Your child. Thank You for grafting me into the family and making me Your own. Thank You for calling me special. And most of all, thank You for loving me enough to send Your Son to die for me. Amen.

Day 271

GODLY MARRIAGE

Each one of you also must love his wife as he loves himself, and the wife must respect her husband.

EPHESIANS 5:33 NIV

Marriage is a reciprocal relationship. For it to work well, both parties have to give and receive. If you share house space without the love and respect that make it a home, yours quickly becomes an empty existence. But that's not what God had in mind when He created marriage to reflect His own love for His people. He can help your marriage shine brightly for Him, if only you ask Him and are open to His will.

PRAYER

I love Your thoughts on marriage, Lord. I love the back-and-forth movement of husband and wife, each giving and each receiving. You really show Your heart for us through this special union. Marriage is to serve as a genuine reflection of You. Today I pray for all of those who are married, that they would be able to walk in this sort of union. And for those who aren't married but want to be, I pray for godly partners who will help them become all they're meant to be. Thank You for godly marriage, Lord! Amen.

Day 272

JETS AND SUBMARINES

No power in the sky above or in the earth below. . .
will ever be able to separate us from the love of
God that is revealed in Christ Jesus our Lord.
ROMANS 8:39 NLT

Have you ever been diving amid the spectacular array of vivid color and teeming life in the silent world under the sea? Myriad fish painted rainbow hues are backlit by diffused sunbeams. Multi-textured coral dot the gleaming white sand. You honestly feel as if you're in another world. But every world is God's world. He soars above the clouds with us and spans the depths of the seas. Nothing can separate us from His love.

PRAYER

I'm so grateful nothing can separate me from Your love, Lord God. It's far too vast, immeasurable, beyond anything I could imagine. It's bluer than the bluest sky, deeper than the deepest ocean, and higher than any mountain peak. I didn't have to do anything to earn this love. You simply lavish it on me because I'm Your child. And I am as precious to You as any other of Your creations, even the loveliest of them. I'm not sure how to go about thanking You for this love, except to respond in kind. I love You, Lord! Amen.

Day 273

THE PRICE OF FORGIVENESS

And according to the law almost all things are purified with blood, and without shedding of blood there is no remission.
HEBREWS 9:22 NKJV

Many people in our world would like cheap forgiveness. They want someone to say they are okay, but they don't want to pay any price for their wrongdoing. That's not how forgiveness works according to the Bible, though. Remission of sins comes at a high price: sacrificial blood, the blood of Jesus. Jesus says that you are worth this expense and that you are clean in Him. Put away sin and rejoice in His deep love for you.

PRAYER

Some things come at a very high price, don't they, Lord? Houses. Cars. Decisions. I've paid the price more times than I can remember—and not just financially. The same is true when I've messed up. I'd rather just move on and forget about it. But there are times when You call me not just to apologize but to make restitution. It's humbling, for sure, but I want to please Your heart and do right by the other person. So I will humble myself, accept Your forgiveness, and take positive steps to make things right. Thank You for being a forgiving God! Amen.

Day 274

PICK ME UP, DADDY

We celebrate in hope of the glory of God.

Romans 5:2 NASB

To rejoice means to live joyfully. . .joy-fully. . .full of joy. Joy is a decision we make. A choice not to keep wallowing in the mud of our lives. And there will be mud—at one time or another. When spiritual rain mixes with the dirt of fallen people, mud is the inevitable result. The Creator of sparkling sunbeams, soaring eagles, and spectacular fuchsia sunsets wants to lift us out of the mud. Why don't we raise our arms to Him today?

PRAYER

Sometimes I really do feel like I'm stuck in the mud, Lord. I'm bogged down, unable to put one foot in front of the other. The enemy has me bound. But You? You see me as a soaring eagle, not a mud dweller. You are showing me how to rise above the muddy circumstances of my life and lift my arms in praise. Once I'm cleansed of the grime, I'm free to soar. And that's exactly what I want to do with the rest of my life, Father! May I be all You've called me to be! Amen.

Day 275

PASS IT ON

"If you forgive other people for their offenses, your heavenly Father will also forgive you."
MATTHEW 6:14 NASB

Forgiveness isn't only something God gives us. He designed it to be passed on to others. As we do so, we learn the value of the pardon the Father has offered us. Even when everything in us screams, "No, I can't forgive," He empowers us to do so if we trust in Him. Our loving Father never commands us to do anything He will not also strengthen us to do.

PRAYER

A spark can set a whole field ablaze, Lord. And that's how it is with forgiveness. You've forgiven me so that I can turn around and offer the same grace to others who have wronged me. No matter the crime they committed. No matter how bad it made me feel. You want me to pardon in the same way that You pardon: without question. That doesn't mean I need to stay in harmful relationships, but it does mean that I release this person so they no longer have control over my thoughts or my heart. Thank You for setting me free so that I can set others free! Amen.

Day 276

HIS HEART'S DELIGHT

The Lord's delight is in those who fear him,
those who put their hope in his unfailing love.
Psalm 147:11 NLT

Do you remember how you felt when you witnessed your baby's first faltering steps? Delight. That's what it was. Just like when you heard her sing "Jesus Loves Me" in her squeaky, off-key voice, or when she served you tea in tiny pink teacups. The Bible says the Lord delights in us, His children, the very same way. We warm His heart and bring a smile to His lips when we honor Him with our lives. May we long to delight Him in everything we say and do.

PRAYER

How I love this imagery, Lord! I find such delight in the things a little child does—from those adorable little giggles to the sing-songy voice. You really knew what You were doing when You created kids! I definitely adore them. It's so fun to think that You look at me the same way I look at those little ones. You delight in me. You're tickled by me. You get a kick out of me. The way I sing. The way I interact with others. The goofy jokes. The silly smiles. You love every single thing about me. . .and I'm so thrilled to love You back! Amen.

Day 277

THE IMPORTANCE OF FRIENDSHIP

Do not forsake your friend or a friend of your family, and do not go to your relative's house when disaster strikes you—better a neighbor nearby than a relative far away.

PROVERBS 27:10 NIV

Friendship is important to God; otherwise He wouldn't encourage us to hold fast to it. As Christians, we've known times when other believers seemed closer than our kin. God has brought us into a new family—His own—where faith becomes more important than blood. Through Him our love expands, and we help each other when trouble strikes. No matter where you go, God's people are near.

PRAYER

You have definitely surrounded me with amazing friends and loved ones, Lord. I'm so grateful for their comfort, their input, and the special way they've swept me into the fold. May I be loving and welcoming to others as well so that they can sense Your presence. May I be near to those who are hurting, ready with a plate of cookies, strong shoulders, and a few hours of free, uninterrupted time. This is what the body of Christ is like, and I'm so grateful to be part of the family! Thanks for holding us close. Amen.

Day 278

REST STOP

So let's not allow ourselves to get fatigued doing good. At the right time we will harvest a good crop if we don't give up, or quit.
GALATIANS 6:9 MSG

As women, we're used to serving others. It's part of the feminine package. But sometimes we get burned out. Fatigued. Overburdened. Girls, God doesn't want us to be washed-out dishrags, to be so boggled that we try to use our frequent-shopper card at the ATM. It's up to us to recognize the symptoms and rest, regroup, reenergize. This time of refreshing is not indulgent; it's necessary for us to do our best in His name. So give yourself permission to rest. Today.

PRAYER

I feel like I need permission to rest sometimes, Lord. Life is moving so crazy-fast that I can't keep up. And when I see the rapid clip my friends and loved ones are moving at, I feel compelled to have a similar pace. But You're convincing me that I don't need to wear myself out or run myself ragged. You're reminding me that downtime, quiet time, is a good thing. I need that time away from the chaos to regroup and to get my energy level back up. Thanks for taking care of me. . .the whole me. Amen.

Day 279

OUR BEST FRIEND

The righteous choose their friends carefully,
but the way of the wicked leads them astray.
PROVERBS 12:26 NIV

We need friends. Some friends will lead us into trouble, while others will encourage us and lift us up in our faith, drawing us ever nearer to God. Before we get close to others, do we consider their spiritual impact on us? If God is our best friend, let us be cautious not to be led astray. When we share friendship with Jesus with our earthly friends, we are truly blessed.

PRAYER

I've had to tiptoe through this friendship thing with great caution at times, Lord. Sometimes the ones who look like they're a perfect friend-match turn out to be anything but. They drag me down. They pull me into situations I don't want to be a part of. And worst of all, they monopolize my time, drawing me away from the ones who really do build me up. Thank You for the reminder that I need to be cautious about those I include in my inner circle. Help me do a better job of that, I pray. Amen.

Day 280

BATTLE PLAN

I sought the Lord *and He answered me,*
and rescued me from all my fears.
Psalm 34:4 NASB

Nothing is more wasteful than fear. Fear paralyzes, destroys potential, and shatters hope. It's like an enemy attacking from our blind side. But we don't have to allow fear to defeat us. It's a war we can win! First comes earnest prayer; then comes change. God will deliver us from our fears if we seek Him and follow His battle plan.

PRAYER

Fear has locked me in place many times, Lord. I couldn't seem to move forward. My feet were cemented into the pavement, my heart beating a hundred miles an hour. Then, suddenly, Your peace swept over me supernaturally. The fear dissipated. . .and all that was left? Your presence. Your awesome, holy presence. And in those moments, I knew. I knew that You would take care of me. You would deliver me. You would somehow get me through the battle. How grateful I am that You carried me through! Amen.

Day 281

LOVING CORRECTION

For whom the Lord loves He corrects,
just as a father the son in whom he delights.
Proverbs 3:12 NKJV

Do you feel the pain of God's correction? Take heart, knowing it shows that He loves you. Just as a loving father will not let his child walk in a dangerous place, your heavenly Father is redirecting you onto another path. Today's discipline may hurt, but in days to come, your sorrow will turn to joy as you reap the blessing that follows obedience. Your Father loves you deeply.

PRAYER

It's never fun to be corrected, Lord. I'm not a fan. But I know that without correction, my life would veer so far off course that it would be difficult to get back on track again. So I'll take those little nudges. I'll make the necessary adjustments in the moment so I don't end up miles away from where I need to be. And I won't whine and complain or kick back, either. I'll simply trust that You know better than I do and that You have my best interests at heart. You correct me because You love me, and that does my heart good. Amen.

Day 282

TRUMPED

The L*ORD said to Abraham, "Why did Sarah laugh, saying, 'Shall I actually give birth to a child, when I am so old?' Is anything too difficult for the* L*ORD?"*

GENESIS 18:13–14 NASB

Sarah, well past menopause and losing the drooping appendage war, was so floored when told of her impending pregnancy that she burst into laughter. How absurd to think that those breasts sagging to her navel would nurse a baby! But that's exactly what God had in store. We sometimes forget that God created the systems we consider absolute and impenetrable. He can trump them all with a flick of His pinkie!

PRAYER

Nothing is too difficult for You, Lord. You are sovereign. You know all. You see all. And You even see how things are going to end up. Even when things feel absolutely impossible to me—and that happens often—You have ways that are far greater. You pull off miracles with the blink of an eye. And I marvel at all that You accomplish! So please help me when my faith wanes. May it strengthen as I remember that You are for me, not against me. I know You have big plans for my life, things I have yet to see. I can't wait! Amen.

Day 283

HE LOVES YOU!

What great love the Father has lavished on us, that we should be called children of God! And that is what we are!

1 JOHN 3:1 NIV

God doesn't give His love in dribs and drabs. He lavishes it on us when we come to Him in faith. All along, He was waiting to make us His children, and we were the ones who resisted. But once we surrender to Him and He adopts us as His children, God's love lets loose in our lives. Nothing is too good for His obedient children. Praise God that He loves you so much!

PRAYER

I feel it, Lord! I feel that love You're lavishing on me. It's sustaining me, comforting me, giving me courage. Just one of the perks of being Your kid, I guess. And You'll go right on loving me, no matter how I respond. There have definitely been times when I've resisted Your affections. I wanted my own way. I wanted to be left alone. But You kept on, in that gently persuasive way of Yours, finally winning me over. I'll never be able to thank You enough for not giving up on me and for continuing to lavish me with Your remarkable love! Amen.

Day 284

ONE FOR ALL

All of you are part of the same body. There is only one Spirit of God, just as you were given one hope when you were chosen to be God's people.

EPHESIANS 4:4 CEV

Remember the motto of the Three Musketeers? "All for one and one for all." Christ followers should have the same sense of unity, for we are bound together by eternal hope, the gift of our Savior. Feeling with and for each other, we'll cry tears of joy from one eye and tears of sadness from the other. Loneliness is not an option. Take the first step. Reach out today—someone else's hand is reaching out too.

PRAYER

Unity isn't always easy to achieve, Lord. In fact, I often find myself in the middle of squabbles and disagreements with my Christian friends. It's hard to get everyone on the same page. But You want us to try. You want us to come together and merge our efforts on the things we agree on. And You, Lord? You're the thing we agree on. So I'll keep fighting for my relationships. Give me healthy, strong ones, I pray. Show me who needs Your love. And keep on teaching me to walk in unity, even with the ones who are harder to get along with. Amen.

Day 285

ALWAYS FAITHFUL

I will never leave thee, nor forsake thee.
HEBREWS 13:5 KJV

When you're challenged by fear or stress, you need never deal with it single-handedly if Jesus is your Lord. When your life seems in shambles around you, He offers strength and comfort for your hurting heart. God never gives up on you. His love cannot change. Today, delight in the one who never deserts you.

PRAYER

I do look at the rubble around me on occasion, Lord, and wonder how I can keep going on. It seems impossible to crawl out from under it and create some semblance of a new life, a new road. But somehow You give me strength to do just that, even when it feels impossible. My arms gain strength to keep lifting. My legs are empowered to keep walking. And my mouth somehow manages to produce a few meager words of praise and hope. It's all because of You, Lord. So today I want to pause to thank You for never letting me give up. Amen.

Day 286

THEY'RE JUST MEN

"He may have a great army, but they are merely men. We have the Lord *our God to help us and to fight our battles for us!"*
2 Chronicles 32:8 NLT

When facing attack from an enemy army, Hezekiah uttered these profound words: "They're just men. The God of all creation is standing by to fight for us! No comparison!" And sure enough, against all human reasoning, God sent an angel to defeat the entire enemy army (2 Chronicles 32:21). God still intervenes today to help us fight our battles, whether supernaturally or by natural means. Trust Him. He's got His armor on.

PRAYER

It's wonderful to be reminded that "they're just men," Lord. Those who have risen up against me? They don't have a fraction of the power that You possess. And You are for me, not against me, so I have nothing to worry about when they rear their heads! The next time I feel overpowered by the enemy (or those he is using to get me down), please remind me of this scripture. My enemies don't stand a chance against the mighty Creator of all! You can defeat whole armies with just a word. What a wonderful, powerful God You are! Amen.

Day 287

NOTHING IS IMPOSSIBLE

"For nothing will be impossible with God."

LUKE 1:37 NASB

The angel spoke these words to Mary as he gave her the news that the aged Elizabeth would bear a child. God does the impossible in our lives too. We don't bear a Savior, but how has He helped us understand impossible relationships, juggle a hectic schedule, or bring hope to a hurting friend? God offers supernatural support no matter what we face. Nothing is impossible for the one at work in our lives. What impossibilities can He deal with in your life? Have you trusted Him for help?

PRAYER

"It's impossible." "No way." I've used those words a lot, Lord. I get overwhelmed when I look at a mountain looming in front of me, and my very first reaction is to give up. You, though? You don't give up. You look at mountains as nothing more than pebbles. And You ask me to speak to them—using the power of Jesus' name—and watch them tumble to the ground. So today I do that. I speak to the mountains and remind myself that nothing—absolutely nothing—is impossible with my God! Amen.

Day 288

BFFS

I am counting on the L*ORD; yes, I am counting on him. I have put my hope in his word.*

PSALM 130:5 NLT

"Best Friends Forever" earn this title of honor because we've learned we can count on them. They've proven they'll be there for us whether we're svelte or bloated, sweet or grumpy, thoughtful or insensitive. Bailing us out of countless sinking dinghies, they've held us as we sobbed, fed our families, watched our kids, and made us smile. How much more can we count on our Creator to be there for us?

PRAYER

I love my friends, Lord. They've seen me in every circumstance and love me anyway. They were there when I made mistakes, said things I shouldn't have, or messed up in even bigger ways. And yet they've stuck with me. When I think about their dedication, I marvel! And it's just a fraction of the dedication You've shown me, Lord. You've truly stuck with me—You even pursued me in my sinful state, when I turned my back on You and chose sin over You. You simply wouldn't let me go. Thank You for never giving up on me. Amen.

Day 289

GOD OFFERS HOPE

"For I know the plans I have for you," declares the LORD, "plans to prosper you and not to harm you, plans to give you hope and a future."

JEREMIAH 29:11 NIV

As Judah headed into exile, conquered by a savage pagan people, God offered His people hope. He still had a good plan for them, one that would come out of their suffering. Their prosperity was not at an end, though their path through hardship had just begun.

When God leads you up a rocky path, your hope and future remain secure in Him. Faithful trust is all He asks of you.

PRAYER

When I trust Your plans for my life, my hope remains intact, Lord. But when I begin to doubt those plans? Well, I fall off the faith-wagon! I find myself floundering. I wonder if You're even there at all. Thank You for the reminder that Your plans for me are good and that suffering will end. It might not end on this side of heaven, but a day is coming when trials will be nothing more than a memory. Even in exile, You offer hope. Even in pain and suffering, You have plans. May I never forget. Amen.

Day 290

GO FOR IT

When everything was hopeless, Abraham believed anyway, deciding to live. . .on what God said he would do.

ROMANS 4:18 MSG

"You can't do that. It's impossible." Has anyone ever said these words to you? Or have you said them to yourself because of fear or a previous experience with failure?

This world is full of those who discourage rather than encourage. If we believe them, we'll never do anything. But if we, like Abraham, believe that God has called us for a particular purpose, we'll go for it despite our track record. Past failure doesn't dictate future failure. If God wills it, He fulfills it.

PRAYER

You've called me to a purpose, Lord. Sure, I've gotten off track a few times. And yes, I've been discouraged a time or two, thinking things weren't going to work out. But today I'm placing my confidence fully in You, trusting that You're going to work out all of the necessary details to get me where I need to go. In spite of my mistakes, in spite of my weak faith, You can still use me, Lord. Fulfill Your plans in me today, I pray. Amen.

Day 291

A PURPOSEFUL PLAN

And we know that all things work together for good to those who love God, to those who are the called according to His purpose.

ROMANS 8:28 NKJV

Life doesn't always look ideal to us. When finances are tight, family problems are serious, or things just don't seem to go our way, we may doubt that God is working in our lives. That's the time we need to reread this verse and take heart. Even things that don't seem good have a purpose in God's plan. As Christians, we can trust in Him, even when life is less than perfect.

PRAYER

If I didn't know in my heart that You were working a plan, I would be plenty worried, Lord. I would wonder, based solely on circumstances, if perhaps chaos had taken over. But You are working a plan. Many of them, in fact. And if anyone can hold things together, You can. You're not just the activator; You're the glue. And because I know that You know all things, I can trust You to keep working them out for my good and Your glory. Even when things don't look ideal. Even when things are far from perfect. Even then. Amen.

Day 292

HEADING HOME

We are only foreigners living here on earth for a while.
1 CHRONICLES 29:15 CEV

I quivered on the icy Alps peak, more from fear than cold. Which ski slopes were my level (beginner), and which were treacherously advanced? A mistake could be deadly. Panic gripped me; I couldn't read the German signs, and no one spoke English.

As Christians, we're foreigners on this earth. We don't speak the same language or share the same perspective as nonbelievers. We're only passing through this world on our way to the next. . .heading home.

PRAYER

We are strangers here, Lord. No wonder I feel like I don't fit in. This modern culture? It eludes me. . .and that's a good thing. I wouldn't want to "connect" with it. In fact, the crazier things get, the more I long for the bliss of heaven. There's a reason I don't fit in: I'm a spiritual being, created in Your image and born again by Your Spirit. Sure, I live in this earthly body, but one day it too will be gone. Until then, show me how to navigate this life the best I can, sharing Your love and hope with others. Amen.

Day 293

OPEN DOOR

For God so loved the world that he gave his one and only Son, that whoever believes in him shall not perish but have eternal life.

JOHN 3:16 NIV

These words are God's open door to those who believe in His Son. The barrier between God's holiness and man's sinfulness disintegrates when we believe in and accept Jesus' sacrifice for our sin. But we must walk through that open door, by faith, to inherit the eternal life God offers. Have you taken that step, or are you still outside the door?

PRAYER

I've walked through that door, Lord, and I'm so grateful. Here on the other side, I can see so clearly all that You've done for me. You sent Your Son, knowing He would die. That sacrifice on the cross changed not only my life but the lives of billions of people who one day are going to be my neighbors in heaven! When I accepted Jesus, I took on a whole new life and gained a community of believers as friends. Thank You for that open door, Lord. Thank You for loving us enough to give Your all. Amen.

Day 294

I DO

Let us hold unswervingly to the hope we profess, for he who promised is faithful.

HEBREWS 10:23 NIV

An important part of any marriage is the vow of faithfulness. We pledge that we will remain faithful to our beloved until death do us part. Faithfulness is crucial to a trusting relationship. We must be able to depend on our spouse to always be in our corner, to love us even when we're unlovable, and to never leave or forsake us.

God is faithful. We can absolutely count on Him to never break His promises.

PRAYER

Thank You for Your faithfulness, Lord! Thank You for never going back on Your promises, not even once! You're far more trustworthy than even the best human I know, and I know some good ones! Because You're so dependable, I know I can safely put my trust in You no matter how hard the circumstances. I don't have to wonder if You're going to let me down. That would never happen! May I learn from You and grow to be more steadfast and faithful—to You and to others. Amen.

Day 295

GIFT OF LOVE

The LORD takes delight in his people.

PSALM 149:4 NIV

God doesn't just like you—He delights in you. You are so special to Him that He brought you into His salvation so He could spend eternity with you. God loves each of His children in a special way. You aren't just another in a long line of His people. He knows every bit of you, your faithfulness and failures, and loves each part of you "to pieces." We could never earn such love—it is His special gift to each of us. Let's rejoice in that blessing today.

PRAYER

I know what it's like to delight over a child, Lord. I've done it plenty of times with the little ones in my life! I love to see their quirky expressions and feel my heart flood with joy as they laugh and play. Is that how You feel when You look at me? Are you tickled to see my antics? I'm so glad I'm Your child, loved and adored by You. My heart sings with the knowledge that I bring You joy and that You're glad I'm part of the family. Thanks for loving me so well, Lord. Amen.

Day 296

UNFATHOMABLE GRACE

Jesus treated us much better than we deserve. He made us acceptable to God and gave us the hope of eternal life.
TITUS 3:7 CEV

Whereas justice is getting what we deserve and mercy is not getting what we deserve, grace is getting what we don't deserve. Thankfully, God doesn't automatically dole out justice for our myriad sins but rather reaches beyond to mercy—and even a step further to grace. As Jean Valjean discovers in the classic story *Les Miserables*, when we truly grasp God's unfathomable mercy and grace, we are then empowered to extend it to others.

PRAYER

I'm so grateful You didn't give me what I deserved, Lord. You didn't dole out justice for my sins. Instead, You offered grace and forgiveness. And You keep offering it, even now, when I make mistakes. Mercy is who You are! Forgiveness is what You do. I can't begin to comprehend this sort of mercy, but I want to be able to pass it on to others. In other words, I want to be more like You! Please help me with this, I pray. May I withhold vengeance and extend grace, Lord, even when it's hard. Amen.

Day 297

GOD'S LOVE AT WORK

We have known and believed the love that God has for us. God is love, and he who abides in love abides in God, and God in him.

1 JOHN 4:16 NKJV

Trusting in Jesus, you have felt God's love at work in your inner being. The vibrant connection that only Christians experience becomes the center of your life. If you're faithful to abide in Him, His eternal life renews you from head to toe and shines forth radiantly, and your Spirit-inspired words and actions portray God's love to the world.

PRAYER

I would never make it one day without Your love, Lord. It's the spark that keeps me going, day in and day out. You have truly transformed me and made me in Your likeness so that I can live a vibrant and exciting life for You. So I will go on thanking You and sharing the news of what You've done for me so that others can experience this journey too. Trusting in You is by far the best decision I've ever made. Thank You for coming to dwell inside of me! Amen.

Day 298

ROLL DOWN THE WINDOW

"Ask and it will be given to you; seek and you will find; knock and the door will be opened to you."

LUKE 11:9 NIV

Does your significant other have trouble asking for directions? Do you cruise about the country on a scenic tour that could have been avoided by asking a simple question? Asking for help is difficult for all of us to some degree. But that's how we reach our final destinations—and not just on the highway. God offers help if we only ask. He's standing there holding the road map. We just have to stop and roll down the window.

PRAYER

You've always been so patient and kind with me, Lord. You don't rush me along or insist I see things Your way. Instead, You gently guide and—often with just a whisper of Your Spirit—nudge me in the right direction when I'm going astray. Forgive me for the times I haven't asked for help. Thank You for the grace You've offered when I've messed up. Most of all, thank You for the plans You've set in motion for my life. This is a highway I'm safe on, as long as I let You lead the way. Amen.

Day 299

ENDURANCE

As you know, we count as blessed those who have persevered. You have heard of Job's perseverance and have seen what the Lord finally brought about. The Lord is full of compassion and mercy.

JAMES 5:11 NIV

Endurance in faith, hard as it may seem, brings happiness. Trials are not a sign of God's disfavor or His will to carelessly punish His children. The tenderhearted Savior never acts cruelly. But through troubles, we draw close to Him and see God's power at work in our lives. Then, like Job, when we persevere in faith, God rewards us bountifully.

PRAYER

When I think of all that Job endured, my woes pale in comparison. He really went through some difficult times, Lord. Job set an amazing endurance record, that's for sure! No one I know even comes close, though I've certainly whined enough that my friends think I have. The truth is, I'm so grateful for Your presence during the hard times in my life. These seasons are a little less painful when I recognize Your great love and care for me. And I'm even happy for the trials I've been through, Lord, because they've drawn me closer to You. Thank You! Amen.

Day 300

SET FREE

Rahab the prostitute. . . , Joshua spared. . .because she hid the messengers whom Joshua sent to spy out Jericho.

JOSHUA 6:25 NASB

Rahab was the unlikeliest of heroes: a prostitute who sold her body in the darkest shadows. Yet she was the very person God chose to fulfill His prophecy. How astoundingly freeing! Especially for those of us ashamed of our past. God loved Rahab for who she was—not for what she did. Rahab is proof that God can and will use anyone for His higher purposes. Anyone. Even you and me.

PRAYER

I'm so grateful You're not holding my past against me, Lord. I don't want my past indiscretions to affect my relationship with You. Not only have You set me free, but You've given me a new path to walk, a hopeful one filled with possibilities. You want to use me to draw others to You. What an honor that is! It's hard to understand how You can use me like You do, but I'm grateful for the opportunity! Thanks for setting me free from my past to walk in newness of life, Lord. Amen.

Day 301

MERCY TRIUMPHS

Mercy triumphs over judgment.
JAMES 2:13 NIV

Not only is God merciful to us, but He expects us to pass that blessing on to others. Instead of becoming the rule enforcers in this world, we're to paint a picture of the tender love He has for fallen people and to call many other sinners into His love. When we only criticize the world and fail to show compassion, we lose the powerful witness we were meant to have. As you stand firm for Jesus, may mercy also triumph in your life.

PRAYER

I'm not always the most merciful person, Lord. Sometimes—just keeping it real—I roll my eyes instead of engaging with the one who's hurting. Some personalities are harder than others to connect with, but that's no excuse. I want to be more like You, so please help me extend mercy to those who are hurting, even those who rub me the wrong way. I don't want to turn a blind eye or, worse, criticize unnecessarily. Instead, give me a true heart of compassion, one that instantly engages with the hurting and the lost. Amen.

Day 302

NAME ABOVE ALL NAMES

O God, we give glory to you all day long
and constantly praise your name.
PSALM 44:8 NLT

So what has God done that deserves our everlasting praise? His descriptive names tell the story: "a friend who sticks closer than a brother" (Proverbs 18:24 NIV), "altogether lovely" (Song of Solomon 5:16 NIV), "the rock that is higher than I" (Psalm 61:2 NIV), "my strength and my song" (Isaiah 12:2 NLT), "the lifter of my head" (Psalm 3:3 ESV), "shade from the heat" (Isaiah 25:4 ESV). . . His very name fills us with hope!

PRAYER

The list of what You've done and who You've been to me goes on and on, Lord! I can't keep track, the blessings are so many! And I've done nothing to deserve any of these things, other than loving You, which I do with my whole heart. I'm so grateful to You today. I lift praises to Your name: My provider. My salvation. My healer. My comforter. My all in all. My rock. My strength. My hope. My everything! Where would I be without You? Lost and alone. But thanks to Your grace, I have the joy of walking with You every minute of every day. Praise You! Amen.

Day 303

REBIRTH AND RENEWAL

He saved us, not because of righteous things we had done, but because of his mercy. He saved us through the washing of rebirth and renewal by the Holy Spirit.

TITUS 3:5 NIV

Could we save ourselves? No way! Even our best efforts fall far short of God's perfection. If God had left us on our own, we'd be eternally separated from Him. But graciously, the Father reached down to us through His Son, giving Jesus as a sacrifice on the cross. Then the Spirit touched our lives in rebirth and renewal. Together, the three Persons of the Godhead saved us in merciful love.

PRAYER

I'm a fixer, Lord. I like to make things right. But when it comes to my own sin, there's nothing I can do to wash it away. You sent Your Son to do what I could not do. My best efforts couldn't even come close to Jesus' sacrifice on the cross. All of my hard work wouldn't even make a dent. On my own, I'd be separated from You no matter how hard I tried to fix my sin problem. But You, my gracious Lord, changed everything through Your mercy and grace. I'm so grateful for Your gift of salvation! Amen.

Day 304

FEEL THE LOVE

Long before he laid down earth's foundations,
he had us in mind, had settled on us as the focus of
his love, to be made whole and holy by his love.

EPHESIANS 1:4 MSG

Need a boost of hope today? Read this passage aloud, inserting your name for each "us." Wow! Doesn't that bring home the message of God's incredible, extravagant, customized love for you? I am the focus of His love, and I bask in the hope of the healing, wholeness, and holiness that His individualized attention brings. You too, dear sister, are His focus. Allow yourself to feel the love today.

PRAYER

I'm so grateful to understand that You had me in mind all along, Lord. You see me. You care about me. You have plans for me. Your heart is for me, not against me. And because You know me better than anyone else, I can trust You completely with the rest of my days. I don't have to wonder, "Does God even care?" You've proven time and time again that You do. Thank You for focusing so much time on me and for intervening in my life. Thank You for the gifts You give and the wholeness You bring. I am Your contented child! Amen.

Day 305

GOD MEETS OUR NEEDS

"He has brought down rulers from their thrones but has lifted up the humble. He has filled the hungry with good things but has sent the rich away empty."

LUKE 1:52–53 NIV

God provides for every one of His children, even the humblest. Wealth cannot gain His favor nor poverty preclude it. The Father looks not at the pocketbook but at the heart. Those who love Him, though they may lack cash, see their needs fulfilled, but unbelievers who own overflowing storehouses harvest empty hearts. God never ignores His children's needs. What has He given you today?

PRAYER

You've given me everything I need, Lord! Air to breathe. Water to drink. Food to eat. A roof over my head. Transportation. Friends and family to love. A community of people surrounding me. Truly, You've thought of everything. And I don't want to take any of it for granted. I'm so grateful You don't look at my pocketbook, my financial limitations. I'm short on cash but long on faith, hope, and love. And because of You, I know my storehouses will always be full. Thank You for always making provision for me, Lord. Amen.

Day 306

SEEKING AN OASIS

He turns a wilderness into a pool of water,
and a dry land into springs of water.
PSALM 107:35 NASB

The wilderness of Israel is truly a barren wasteland—nothing but rocks and parched sand stretching as far as the distant horizon. The life-and-death contrast between stark desert and pools of oasis water is startling.

Our lives can feel parched too. Colorless. Devoid of life. But God has the power to transform desert lives into gurgling, spring-of-water lives. Ask Him to bubble up springs of hope within you today.

PRAYER

I've been through so many parched seasons, Lord. Honestly? I wondered if I would ever feel moisture on my lips again. When I'm dried up, I feel far away from You. But You always manage to come near, in that supernatural way of Yours, and flood my soul with cool, refreshing rain just when I need it most. You bring life where there was no life, hope where there was no hope, and peace where there was no peace. And Your timing, Lord? It's perfect, as always! Thank You for raining down on me. Amen.

Day 307

HE WILL NEVER FAIL

You open your hand and satisfy the
desires of every living thing.
PSALM 145:16 NIV

Our faithful Lord provides for all His created beings. Will He fail to care for you? How could He satisfy the needs of the smallest birds and beasts yet forget His human child? God is always faithful. Though we fail, He will not. He cannot forget His promises of love and will never forget to provide for your every need.

PRAYER

You love all of creation, Lord, from the tiniest living thing to me, Your child. When a butterfly takes flight, You notice. When a river rages, You see. And when I stumble and fall, You not only observe my troubled state but step directly into it and pick me up. It's so obvious that You love me. And even more, You find great value in me. You say that I will do amazing things with my life. And when You speak such a promise over me, Lord. . .I believe it. Thanks so much for caring for me and for all of Your creation! Amen.

Day 308

FOREVER AND ALWAYS

"Never will I leave you; never will I forsake you."
HEBREWS 13:5 NIV

Unconditional love. We all yearn for it—from our parents, our spouses, our children, our friends. Love based not on our performance or accomplishments but on who we are deep down beneath the fluff. God promises unconditional love to those who honor Him. We don't need to worry about disappointing Him when He gets to know us better—He knows us already. Better than we know ourselves. And He loves us anyway, forever and always.

PRAYER

I love the word *accomplished.* I like when people say, "Wow, you're really good at. . ." and then go on to share how great I am at a particular thing. It feels good to be noticed. To be admired. That said, it feels even better when someone loves me just for me. When they wrap their arms around me simply because I exist. Because they care. You're like that, Lord. You're not waiting for me to do something remarkable before showing me Your love. Every minute of every day, You offer it, no matter what I do—or don't do. Thank You! Amen.

Day 309

GOD'S GREATEST GIFT

If, by the trespass of the one man, death reigned through that one man, how much more will those who receive God's abundant provision of grace and of the gift of righteousness reign in life through the one man, Jesus Christ!

ROMANS 5:17 NIV

What greater gift could God give us than His grace? Once, death ruled over us. Now, life in Christ is ours. As we ponder God's compassion, do we appreciate Christ's sacrifice? Any spiritual value we have comes from His gifts. We can never repay Him, but are we living to show how grateful we are?

PRAYER

You're the best gift giver of all, Lord! You gave the ultimate gift—eternal life! No one else on earth can offer such a thing. But You? You've graciously extended Your hand and said, "Come with Me, child. I've got a whole new world for you." And what a world it's going to be! Eternity with You? It's going to be amazing. Blissful. I'll never be able to thank You enough, and I certainly can't repay You for that free gift, but I'll live every day of my life grateful for You and all You've done for me. Thank You, Lord. Amen.

Day 310

LARGE AND IN CHARGE

"In this world you will have trouble.
But take heart! I have overcome the world."
JOHN 16:33 NIV

"Who's in charge here?" Most mothers have had the experience of returning home to a chaos-wrecked house. Toys, books, clothes, and snack wrappers everywhere. "Why isn't [insert correct answer here: your father, the babysitter, Grandma, etc.] in control?"

Our world can sometimes feel chaotic like that. Things appear to be spinning out of control. But we must remember that God is large and in charge. He has a plan.

PRAYER

I'm always grateful for the reminder that You have a plan, Lord, especially in this current day and age when so many things seem to be out of control. The world is off its rocker. People are living in ways that are completely contrary to Your will. And sometimes all the wickedness seems completely overwhelming to me. I wonder if the enemy is going to go on having his way for long. Then I'm reminded that You really are working a bigger plan, one I can't see. And it brings me comfort and hope. Thank You for being an in-charge God! Amen.

Day 311

KNOWING GOD

In the beginning was the Word, and the Word was with God, and the Word was God.

JOHN 1:1 NIV

Want a picture of God's Word? Look to Jesus, the embodiment of everything the Father wanted to say to us. To look to Jesus, we have to read the Book that tells of Him.

Maybe that's why God takes it personally when we decide not to read His Word. We're ignoring His tender commands and pushing aside His love. The Bible is God's way of communicating with His children. How can we know Him without His Word?

PRAYER

Your Word is the most critically important book in my life, Lord, far more than any other bestseller! I couldn't possibly go without It, not even for a moment! It's a guidebook, a love story, a history book, a collection of life-changing testimonials. The Bible is filled with stories of grace, of grit, and of hope—not just for me but for all of humanity! I love to take my inspiration from its pages, and not just because You command me to. It's a living, breathing part of who I am. I could never separate myself from Your Word. Thank You for this gift! Amen.

Day 312

ONLY THE BEST

I have hidden your word in my heart,
that I might not sin against you.
Psalm 119:11 NLT

I adore homemade chicken salad. Honey mustard, sliced grapes, and slivered almonds make it delicious. Quality ingredients produce quality results. It's all poultry, but there's a big difference between white meat and gizzards.

Memorizing scripture is like preparing chicken salad for the soul. God's Word (quality ingredients) will be ready at a moment's notice to guide, comfort, and train us in righteousness (quality results). Anything else is just gizzards.

PRAYER

I've had enough of the gizzards, Lord. I've tasted of what the world has to offer, and it's second-rate, if even that. Your Word is top of the line. Everything else pales in comparison. Thank You for the reminder that I need to memorize scriptures and keep them tucked away in my heart so that they come soaring out when needed. And honestly? They're always needed—morning, noon, and night. Your Word, which I love, is always at the ready, and I'm happy to use it. When I do, mountains move! Amen.

Day 313

FLAWLESS WORDS

"Every word of God is flawless."
PROVERBS 30:5 NIV

Maybe you've had days when you've been tempted to doubt this verse. You wanted to go in one direction, and God's Word said to go in another. But if you were wise, you trusted in its truth instead of following your own way. After all, can you claim that your every word is error-free? No. How much better to follow in the perfect way of your Lord, who willingly shares His wisdom. To avoid many of the snares of this world, trust the flawless Word of God.

PRAYER

Your Holy Word is sheer perfection, Lord God. Thank You for the reminder that we need to treat it as such and not speak about the Bible flippantly. The words we find on its pages are life-giving. They're like panning for—and finding—gold. Only, the Bible's words are ten million times more valuable. More than anything, I want to obtain the kind of wisdom found only in the Bible. It will give me guidance and direction for my life, as well as comfort on the days when things aren't going so well. Thank You for Your Word, Father! Amen.

Day 314

HEALING HEAT

When I am weak, then I am strong.
2 CORINTHIANS 12:10 NASB

As an occupational therapist, I make splints for people with broken bones. The thermoplastic splinting material comes in sheets as hard and unyielding as plywood. When heated, the thermoplastic becomes pliable so it can be cut and molded into a form that promotes healing.

Like that thermoplastic, we're strongest and most usable when we've gone through the molding process. Heat transforms us into malleable beings whom God can use to heal hearts and spirits.

PRAYER

I'm not a fan of going through the fire, Lord, but I've had to face the furnace many times in my life. I can still smell the smoke in my hair! I know these trials make me stronger in the end, but they're sure not fun in the moment! Thank You for the reminder that You're making me pliable and then—ultimately—much stronger. Until then, as I walk through challenges, please give me courage and trust to keep going, even when I don't feel like it. May I never forget that when I am weak, then I am strong—but only when I put my trust in You. Amen.

Day 315

THE LIGHT

When Jesus spoke again to the people, he said, "I am the light of the world. Whoever follows me will never walk in darkness, but will have the light of life."
JOHN 8:12 NIV

Following the light of the world means you can see where you're headed. Even when life becomes confusing and totally dark, your goal hasn't changed and you keep heading in the right direction. When you're walking in Jesus' light, though you may hit a dark patch, you'll remain on the road with the Savior, and in Him you'll always see enough to take the next step.

PRAYER

I can't imagine driving in the dark with no headlights, Lord. I'd drive off the road, no doubt about it. The light guides me to where I need to go. The same is true when I walk with You. This world is a dark, terrifying place. But when You're at my side, I have the Light of the World illuminating the path ahead, showing me which way to move. As long as I stick close to You, I'll never have to worry about walking in the darkness again. Your guiding light brings such peace to my soul. Thank You, Lord! Amen.

Day 316

DID YOU SAY SOMETHING?

"Call to Me and I will answer you, and I will tell you great and mighty things, which you do not know."
JEREMIAH 33:3 NASB

As someone who's been there, done that, I love the commercial in which the husband has his face buried in the newspaper when his wife pops the no-win question: "Does this dress make me look fat?" "You bet," he distractedly replies.

God promises not only to hear us when we call to Him but to answer by teaching us new and amazing things. He's never distracted. He's always listening. And He always cares.

PRAYER

I'm so glad you don't respond flippantly when I cry out to You, Lord. You're so tuned in to me that You hear before I even speak a word. You hear my heart. And You're always ready with an answer for whatever I'm going through. I never have to wonder if You're on the job. You are! I wouldn't blame You if You were distracted taking care of major things going on around the globe, but in addition to handling worldwide concerns, You still have time for each and every one of Your children. What an amazing Father You are! Amen.

Day 317

HOPE IN HIM

Put your hope in God, for I will yet praise him, my Savior and my God.

Psalm 42:5 NIV

Where else should the believer place her hope? No one besides Jesus has the power to turn her life around. No solution lies beyond Him, and He never pushes her away. When the world becomes harsh, she still receives His gentle encouragement.

Though you wait long and the path seems hard, hold on to Jesus. Words of praise will pass your lips as you see His salvation accomplished. Your God will never let you fall.

PRAYER

Over the years I've placed my hope in many things—and people. Family. Friends. My boss. Coworkers. My bank account. My job. My home. My personal belongings. My rank. My title. My talents. My abilities. My prestige. I found myself trusting in all of it. But then I watched as all of those things disappointed me. It didn't always happen on purpose, especially with my loved ones, but I finally figured out that I really can't put my trust in anyone but You. I'm so grateful You've proven Yourself trustworthy all these years, Lord. Amen.

Day 318

IT'S NOT OVER

When the wicked die, their hopes die with them,
for they rely on their own feeble strength.
PROVERBS 11:7 NLT

Tony Dungy, Super Bowl champion, coach, and author of *Quiet Strength*, said, "It's because of God's goodness that we can have hope, both for here and the hereafter."*

Coach Dungy's testimony of eternal hope for those who rely on God's infinite strength touched many hearts after the tragic loss of his teenage son. Death is not the end. There is a hope, a future for those who choose not to rely on their own feeble strength.

PRAYER

I've mourned the deaths of many loved ones, Lord. Most were close to You and were strong believers. I know they're in heaven with You. A few others, I'm not so sure about. My confidence—my hope—isn't as strong. When it's my time to go, I want everyone to know. I don't want anyone fretting, wondering if I'm in heaven or not. May my friends and loved ones have full confidence, based on my walk and my bold testimony, that I'm a child of the most high God. And may I lead as many as I can to You so that they can go to heaven one day too. Amen.

---

* Tony Dungy, *Quiet Strength* (Tyndale, 2007).

Day 319

BE STRONG

Be strong and take heart, all you who hope in the LORD.

PSALM 31:24 NIV

Hope is not some weak, airy-fairy kind of thing. It takes strength to put your trust in God when life batters your heart and soul. Weaklings rarely hold on to positive expectation for long, because it takes too much from them. But the spiritually strong put their trust in God and let Him lift up their hearts in hope. Then battering may come, but it cannot destroy them. Hope makes Christians stronger still.

PRAYER

I can't, but You can. And knowing that You can is a real lifeline for me, Lord. I've faced situations so impossible, so frightening, that it made no sense to keep hanging on to the lifeline; but now, looking back, all I can say is, "Thank God I did!" You somehow gave me hope during those hopeless times. You strengthened me when there was absolutely nothing inside of me that wanted to keep going. And even though I've taken a few beatings, I'm up and running, convinced that You are for me, not against me. Thank You, Lord! Amen.

Day 320

STREETS OF TREATS

What you hope for is kept safe for you in heaven.
COLOSSIANS 1:5 CEV

Heaven. Will the streets really be paved with gold? Or even better—chocolate? If our earthly treasures are our source of security and hope, we're in trouble. Rust, decay, thieves, recession. . .things just aren't safe. But peace? Joy? Celebrating forever in our Lord's presence? All waiting for us safely in heaven. (But who says we can't hope for Godiva-cobbled streets?)

PRAYER

I have a great imagination, Lord. Sometimes I just sit and daydream about what heaven will be like. My imagination takes me a lot further than golden streets and pearly gates. I wonder, will we be teleported from place to place? What will the food taste like? Will I have to cook it? Will my parents recognize me? I could lose myself to the possibilities. Then I realize that the whole point of heaven is spending time with You. Those questions I have? They don't really matter. All that matters is how blessed I am to spend eternity in the bliss of heaven. Amen.

Day 321

OBEDIENCE = JOY

"I have told you this so that my joy may be in you and that your joy may be complete."
JOHN 15:11 NIV

What wouldn't we do to share Jesus' complete joy! But this verse comes after one of Jesus' commands to obedience. Ah, now do we change our minds? Does joy suddenly become impossible? When Jesus calls us to act, do we follow, or do we decide it's too hard and give up immediately? Let's keep our eyes on the outcome—the joy of our Lord filling our lives. Then obedience too may become a joy.

PRAYER

You don't have to tell me twice, Lord! You want my joy to be complete? Me too! And if it ever looks like I'm changing my mind, just give me a gentle nudge in that way You do. I'll come around in no time. Why wouldn't I want to live a joy-filled life? I won't get bogged down in the muck and mire of the problems I'm facing. Instead, I choose to look ahead to the glorious outcomes You have planned for me. Because I know I can trust You, I will keep a smile on my face and a song in my heart. Amen.

Day 322

JUSTICE FOR ALL?

Our God, you save us, and your fearsome deeds answer our prayers for justice!
PSALM 65:5 CEV

It's not fair! How many times have we uttered this indignant cry when life handed us injustice? We demand justice—it's what we deserve, right? But what about all those times we've misstepped or misjudged? James 2:13 tells us that mercy triumphs over judgement. Mercy forgives mistakes and doesn't dole out what is deserved. Mercy—like a jail sentence pardoned. Mercy—like a man on a cross.

PRAYER

I've made a few mistakes along the way, Lord. Judged a little too harshly. Offered opinions a little too loudly. And there were times, I admit, when I let my pride get in the way. Being right was more important than offering grace. But Your way is different. Your way is better. Instead of doling out judgement, You want me to be more merciful. When I think about it, You have been incredibly merciful to me. You've pardoned my sins more than once. So please help me as I offer the same grace to others. Amen.

Day 323

JOY WILL COME

My lips will shout for joy when I sing praise to you—I whom you have delivered.

PSALM 71:23 NIV

Having trouble finding joy in your life today? Do what the psalmists often did and remind yourself of what God has already done for you. How many ways has following Him blessed you? Begin by thanking Him for His saving grace, and you'll jumpstart the joy no matter what you face today. Your lips will reveal the delight in your heart.

PRAYER

Some days I have to choose joy, Lord. And then, on top of that, I have to choose to voice it aloud by praising You when I don't feel like it. I'm learning that I can't go by my feelings. They betray me every time. (And they're so fickle!) I have to acknowledge them and bring them under godly control by submitting them to You. When I'm in a woe-is-me state, a few rounds of praise and gratitude usually turn things around in a hurry. So I choose to praise You today, Lord! You are worthy, no matter what I'm feeling! Amen.

Day 324

SMILING HEARTS

Weeping may last for the night, but a shout of joy comes in the morning.

PSALM 30:5 NASB

What woman hasn't seen the dim underbelly of 2:00 a.m. through hot tears? God gave us emotionally sensitive spirits and is willing to sit with us as we weep through the long, hard night. Sometimes "night" lasts for a season. But He promises that the sun will eventually rise. And on that glorious morning, we'll be filled with so much joy, even our hearts will smile. Joy is appreciated most in the wake of disappointment.

PRAYER

Been there, done that, Lord. And You were the one to talk me down off the ledge. Those middle-of-the-night weep-fests are grueling but sometimes necessary to purge myself of the pain. I feel like I've been through more than my fair share of night seasons, but then I look around me and realize all of my loved ones are going through similar woes. Thank You for bringing joy, even in the middle of the pain. Thank You for dawn's light. And most of all, thank You for hope, which helps see me through those late-night episodes when I feel like things will never work out. Amen.

Day 325

CLOSE TO JESUS

"Be still, and know that I am God."
PSALM 46:10 NIV

So often, we seek to do things for God or to prove our Christian witness. But if we become simply caught up in busyness, we lose the distinction of our faith: a close relationship with Jesus. Knowing God is not about what we do but about who we love. Our good works mean little if we disconnect from Him. Spend time being still with God today, and a deepened knowledge of Him will be your blessing.

PRAYER

"It's not about what I do." I need to pause and really reflect on those words, Lord. I'm such a doer. Go, go, go. Do, do, do. And it's fun to be a go-getter, but sometimes I lean a little too much on my own strength in the process. Thank You for the reminder that You want me to lean on You, to be in such close relationship with You that I learn to let go of my go-getter tendencies and rely on You. I don't need to prove anything—to You or to others. I simply need to be Your child. Thanks for adopting me, Lord! Amen.

Day 326

WHO'S YOUR DADDY?

His name is the Lord. A father to the fatherless. . .is God in his holy dwelling.
Psalm 68:4–5 niv

His father left when my friend Ben was two. Ben recognized him once—from pictures—at a family funeral, but his father intentionally turned away. When Ben was thirty-five, with a family of his own, his father suddenly showed up seeking a relationship. Sadly, he was diagnosed with cancer shortly after their reunion and died within one year. Ben mourned but knew his real paternal relationship was with God, the Father to the fatherless.

PRAYER

What a wonderful Father You are, Lord! Where our earthly dads slack off, You go the distance. You're there in every way a father should be—loving, caring, making provision, showing up. And the relationship You long for with each of Your children is more intense and deeper than we could imagine. That's how much You adore us. It's crazy to think that there are billions of people on the planet and that Your fatherly love extends to all. I don't know how You do it, but I sure am grateful, Abba Father! Amen.

Day 327

KNOW HIM INTIMATELY

"I will take you as my own people, and I will be your God. Then you will know that I am the Lord *your God, who brought you out from under the yoke of the Egyptians."*

Exodus 6:7 NIV

God freed the Hebrews from slavery and brought them to their new land. But He didn't stop there. Today, He still proves Himself to people by freeing them from sin's slavery and creating loving relationships with them. Has God freed you from sin? Then know Him intimately. Draw near and enjoy His blessings, no matter what kind of "slavery" you faced before.

PRAYER

I sometimes wonder if people even realize they're enslaved, Lord. They live all twisted up but don't seem to recognize the spiritual battle taking place around them. My prayer today is that all of my friends and loved ones would be set free from the chains that bind them. You've done it for me, and I know You can do it for them as well. May they rise to walk in new life with you, free of the bondage of sin, addiction, mental struggles, and pain. May You heal from the inside out, Lord, bringing eternal relief. Amen.

Day 328

FRESH AND GREEN

They will still bear fruit in old age,
they will stay fresh and green.
PSALM 92:14 NIV

Doris, a tiny ninety-year-old widow in my Bible study, is teaching me how to be a blessing. That's her prayer every morning of her life: "Lord, make me a blessing to someone today." And sure enough, God uses her to touch lives in His name—helping a frantic woman find her lost keys, taking a sick neighbor to the doctor, offering a friendly word to the grumpy wheelchair-bound man. . . Little blessings are big indeed to those in need.

PRAYER

All my life I've heard the expression "Blessed to be a blessing," Lord. And You've certainly blessed me a lot through the years. So that's my prayer today. Like that ninety-year-old woman, may I start each day with a prayer on my lips to help others. To bless them in fun and unexpected ways. I know You. You'll give me creative ideas. Should I bake cookies? Offer to mow a yard? Drive a friend to the doctor's office? Take her to lunch? There are so many ways to reach out, and I want to be a blessing. Thanks for those nudges, Lord. Amen.

Day 329

FATHER AND SON

We know also that the Son of God has come and has given us understanding, so that we may know him who is true. And we are in him who is true by being in his Son Jesus Christ. He is the true God and eternal life.

1 JOHN 5:20 NIV

How do we know God? Through His Son, Jesus, who helps us understand the love of His Father. There is no space, no difference of opinion, between Father and Son. When we know the Son, we know God truly. Trust in one is trust in both.

PRAYER

Because I know Jesus, I know You, Father. His pure and unselfish love demonstrated on the cross was Your love. The compassion poured out as He healed those in his path was Your compassion. I know You because I love Him. You are one and the same. And because I've put my trust in my Savior, I know I can spend eternity knowing and loving You. The bliss of heaven will be all the greater because I know and love the one who spun the stars into space! Truly my relationship with You is the most amazing relationship of my life. Amen.

Day 330

SUPERWOMAN ISN'T HOME

"But we will devote ourselves to prayer and to the ministry of the word."
ACTS 6:4 NASB

As busy women, we've found out the hard way that we can't do everything. Heaven knows we've tried, but the truth has found us out: Superwoman is a myth. So we must make priorities and focus on the most important. Prayer and God's Word should be our faith priorities. If we only do as much as we can do, then God will take over and do what only He can do. He's got our backs, girls!

PRAYER

I'm so glad Superwoman is a myth, Lord. You know I've tried to be her but have failed miserably! Working around the clock. Tending to family. Fixing meals. Playing chauffeur. Working at my job. Doing laundry. Paying bills. Heading up committees at work and church. Taking on a position with the homeowners association. I've tried to be everything to everyone. . .and it just didn't work. The burnout nearly did me in, and no one was happy in the end, especially not me. Thank You for the reminder that You're not wanting me to be Superwoman. Whew! Amen.

Day 331

PERFECTING OUR LOVE

Jesus replied: "'Love the Lord your God with all your heart and with all your soul and with all your mind.'"
MATTHEW 22:37 NIV

This simple command can be a real challenge, can't it? No matter how we try in our own power to love God completely, we always seem to fail somewhere. Only as God's Spirit works in our hearts will our whole being become ever more faithful. God works in us day by day, perfecting our love. Ask Him to help you love Him today.

PRAYER

It seems weird asking for help to love You, Lord. But I confess I'm not always the most loving child. Sometimes I make things hard on You. I don't appreciate You enough. I don't speak words of love. It takes the presence and power of Your Spirit to woo me, to draw me back. That's sad, really. I shouldn't need an extra nudge to show my love to the one who has saved me, delivered me, and kept me all of these years. Today my heart cries out to You, Father. You are my God. . .and I love You with my whole heart. Amen.

Day 332

HE IS ABLE

The prospect of the righteous is joy.
PROVERBS 10:28 NIV

Living joyfully isn't denying reality. The righteous don't receive a "Get Out of Pain Free" card when they place their trust in Christ. We all have hurts in our lives. Some we think we cannot possibly endure. But even in the midst of our darkest times, our heavenly Father is able to reach in with gentle fingers to touch us and infuse us with joy that defies explanation. Impossible? Perhaps by the world's standards. Yet He is able.

PRAYER

I'm happy to hear that there's no pain or sickness in heaven, Lord. That's the only "Get Out of Pain Free" card You offer, but it's a great one. Right here? Right now? I'm going through some stuff. And it's not easy. Painful, even. There are times when it feels like too much. But I know You're walking this road with me. And I also know that I'm not the only one struggling. I look around and see friends and loved ones on a similar path. Thank You for taking care of us. And thank You that one day, in the bliss of heaven, all of the pain will be gone forever. Amen.

Day 333

A GENTLE REMINDER

If a man say, I love God, and hateth his brother, he is a liar: for he that loveth not his brother whom he hath seen, how can he love God whom he hath not seen?

1 JOHN 4:20 KJV

John's letter is definitely a challenge to us. Now we wonder, *Do I love God at all?* Surely on our own we couldn't. But when we accept Jesus as our Savior and receive the love of the Father, our attitude changes. In Jesus, we can love even a bothersome brother. Sometimes we just need a gentle reminder.

PRAYER

There are a few bothersome brothers in my life, Lord. And a few sisters too. They get under my skin. They annoy me. But when I pause to think it through, I realize that I probably annoy some people too. Maybe they consider me a bother. Thanks for the reminder that even the bothers are a blessing. We are meant to love them all, even the hard cases. I want to be more like You, Lord, and that means extending love to those who—in my estimation—don't deserve it. But You say we're all worthy of love. Thank You for that reminder. Amen.

Day 334

LIGHTHOUSE LOVE

For God, who said, "Light shall shine out of darkness," is the One who has shone in our hearts.

2 CORINTHIANS 4:6 NASB

Have you heard the story of the lighthouse keeper's daughter who kept faithful vigil for her sailor? Every night she watched as the light's beam pierced the blackness and sliced through raging storms, driven by relentless hope that her lover would return to her on the morning's tide. God loves us like that. He's our light in the darkness: guiding, beckoning, and filling our hearts with hope. He never tires. He never stops.

PRAYER

I don't want to make You search too hard for me, Lord! May I never hide too far in the darkness away from You. May my heart always be ready for some time in Your courts. I want to be the bride who yearns for her groom, the one who says, "Here I am!" Your love is the driving force of my life, the most compelling thing I've ever experienced. I can never thank You enough for the way You tenderly care for Your own, Lord. May I always be ready to run into Your arms. Amen.

Day 335

NEW LIFE

Therefore, if anyone is in Christ, he is a new creation; old things have passed away; behold, all things have become new.
2 CORINTHIANS 5:17 NKJV

New life in Christ: what indescribable freedom to be separated from our sin! No longer bound by sin but able to live in Christ, we joyfully race into our new existence.

But in time, our tendency to fall into sin tarnishes God's gift. Suddenly we don't feel so new. "Old" Christians need only turn again to Christ for forgiveness, and the Spirit's cleansing makes us new again.

PRAYER

Sometimes I look at old photographs of my grandparents, now faded and worn. I have to squint to make out the people in the pictures. Time has almost erased what was once clearly visible. That's how it is with my old sins, isn't it, Lord? You've cast them as far as the east is from the west. They've faded from view, not to be seen—or used against me—anymore. Thank You for making all things new. Thank You for your immeasurable forgiveness. And thank You, Lord, for washing me as white as snow. Amen.

Day 336

A GLIMMER OF HOPE

You have placed your faith and hope in God because he raised Christ from the dead and gave him great glory.
1 PETER 1:21 NLT

Have you ever wondered how Mary felt that Easter morning when she discovered Jesus' tomb empty? She was already engulfed in grief, so imagine her shock at discovering the body of her Savior—the one who held all her hopes and dreams—gone! How could that be? Maybe. . . ? Hope glimmers. But no—impossible. He did say something about resurrection, but that was figurative, wasn't it? Who are. . . You are? I must run and tell them. It's true! He has risen! He's alive! My hope lives too!

PRAYER

I've been through so many seasons of despair, Lord. Grief. Agony. Loneliness. Disappointment. There have been low points that felt like forever-places, proverbial sealed tombs. And I wondered if I would be locked away forever. Then, just as Easter morning tipped the scales in mankind's favor, the stone rolled away from my grief. My agony. My pain. You sent ribbons of sunlight into those vast dark places and gave me hope. Gave me peace. Gave me courage to keep going. How I praise You for Your miraculous hope! Amen.

Day 337

CELEBRATE YOUR NEWNESS

If Christ is in you, the body is dead because of sin,
but the Spirit is life because of righteousness.
ROMANS 8:10 NKJV

Know Jesus? Then your body and your fleshly desires are less important than your spirit. Because Jesus lives in you, sin has no permanent claim on your life. Though it tempts you and you may give in for a time, it no longer has a firm grasp on all your days. You can turn aside from it and dwell in your Lord instead. Celebrate your newness in Jesus: Live for Him today!

PRAYER

Sin is a choice. And I'll be honest, I've often made the wrong choice, Lord. I stepped across lines I never should have ventured near. And I paid heavy prices for some of those choices. I'm so grateful that sin no longer has me bound. I don't have to give in to temptation. I can make a better choice, to walk away. It's because You live inside me now, Jesus, that my fleshly desires don't drive me like they used to. You give me power, self-control, and the desire to please Your heart, not myself. Thank You! Amen.

Day 338

WALKIN' BOOTS

I heard about you from others;
now I have seen you with my own eyes.
JOB 42:5 CEV

As children we sang, "Jesus loves me, this I know; for the Bible tells me so," and we believed because, well, we were told to. But we reach a crossroads as adults: Either pull on the boots of faith and take ownership or simply polish them occasionally—maybe at Easter and Christmas—and allow them to sit neglected and dusty in the closet. Have you taken ownership of your faith? Go ahead, sister. Those boots were made for walkin'!

PRAYER

I've always been one of those "I won't believe it till I see it with my own eyes" girls, Lord. I like visible proof. My walk with You? Well, I can honestly say that I've now got the proof—firsthand—that You exist and You are who You say You are. When You interrupted my life with Your love, it compelled me to want to know You more. And when I gave my heart to You? Then I realized that every word I'd read about you in the Bible was 100 percent true. I've taken full ownership of my faith, Lord. I've strapped on my faith-boots and I'm off and running! Amen.

Day 339

DON'T BE AFRAID TO ASK

Brothers and sisters, pray for us.
1 THESSALONIANS 5:25 NIV

Do you find it hard to ask others to pray for you? Don't be afraid to take that step into humility. Paul wasn't when he asked the Thessalonians to pray for his ministry. Being part of the church requires an interdependence of prayers given and received. As members of a congregation pray for each other, their spirits connect in a new, deeper way. Choose carefully those with whom you share private concerns, but never fear to ask a mature Christian to pray for you.

PRAYER

I honestly don't know where I'd be if not for the prayer warriors in my life, Lord. You've strategically placed me in groups of people who really know how to come out swinging on my behalf when I'm hurting. I'm so grateful for each and every one. It's not always easy to share my needs with others, but I'm never sorry in the end. Knowing that others are praying, that they're storming heaven on my behalf? What an honor! Thank You for my praying friends, Lord. Amen.

Day 340

LABOR

We call to mind your work of faith, your labor of love, and your patience of hope in following our Master, Jesus Christ, before God our Father.

1 THESSALONIANS 1:3 MSG

Labor. The word alone draws a shudder from the most stalwart of pregnant women. Just as laboring to bring forth new physical life requires patience, birthing new spiritual life may require an intensive labor of love: ceaseless prayer. Countless women on their knees praying for the salvation of a loved one have rejoiced in answered prayer. Their secret? Patience of hope.

PRAYER

It's interesting to think of *love* and *labor* in the same sentence, Lord. And yet love is often laborious. It takes work. It takes time. But we know—just as we know when labor pains produce a healthy child—that the end result will be worth it. Thank You for helping me love the unlovable. Thanks for never letting me give up on the ones who don't yet know You. And thank You, most of all, for how hard You worked to convince me of Your love for me. My status as Your child is the result of much patience on Your part, and I'm extremely grateful. Amen.

Day 341

THE BEST ANSWER

Pray without ceasing.
1 THESSALONIANS 5:17 KJV

Haven't gotten an answer to your prayer? Don't give up. There's no time limit on speaking to God about your needs. It's just that we often work on a different time schedule from God. We want an answer yesterday, while He has something better in mind for tomorrow. So keep praying. God listens to His children and gives them the best answer, not the fastest one.

PRAYER

I'm pretty tenacious, Lord. You know this about me. I'm not one to stop before I get what I think I want. Thanks for the reminder that I need to be just as tenacious when it comes to prayer. May I stay on my knees, pressing through, until the victory comes. I won't give up, even when You don't answer right away or when You come back with a different plan. Instead, I'll trust You with the situation. You've never let me down before and I know You won't start now. Thanks for reminding me never to give up! Amen.

Day 342

ESSENTIAL TRIO

Love is patient, love is kind.

1 CORINTHIANS 13:4 NIV

Love, patience, and kindness go together. In fact, it's hard to imagine love that would not express itself in both patience and kindness! That's because even intense, God-given love for the people in your life does not protect you from feeling annoyed with them or exasperated by their actions from time to time. Yet true love prompts you to respond through their weakness. True love compels you to treat them with kindness, not malice, when they upset or offend you. Love, patience, kindness—three must-haves for strong, healthy, and lasting relationships.

PRAYER

Could you loan me some of Your patience, Lord? Mine seems to be wearing thin lately. I try. . .and try. . .and try. But eventually I lose my cool and my patience, usually at about the same time. Thank You for the reminder that we don't have to be undone by seasons of waiting. I don't have to be wrecked when I don't get what I want when I want it. Instead, I can use this as a season of growth, faith, and expectation. I'm also grateful for the reminder that You have enough patience for both of us! Amen.

Day 343

BLESSING BEYOND REPENTANCE

"Repent, then, and turn to God, so that your sins may be wiped out, that times of refreshing may come from the Lord."
ACTS 3:19 NIV

When we consider repentance, we tend to think it's hard. That's only because we're shortsighted. Giving up sin may not appeal to our hardened hearts because we're not looking at the blessing beyond repentance. Yet as we turn from sin, we feel the refreshing breath of God's Spirit bringing new life to our bodies, minds, and spirits. Does anything seem difficult then?

PRAYER

I've given up on a lot of things in my life, Lord. Diets. Balanced budgets. Jobs. Friendships. But You don't want me to ever give up on repentance. You long for me to come to You and share my remorse over the things I've done wrong. I never want to break Your heart, so I choose to speak up. I will turn from the things that pull me away from You. Repentance brings blessing, and I'm grateful You're so gentle with me each and every time. Thank You for second chances! Amen.

Day 344

WAIT JUST A MINUTE

We wait in hope for the LORD; he is our help and our shield.

PSALM 33:20 NIV

Impatience: archenemy of women. Like Batman's Riddler or Superman's Lex Luthor, impatience stalks us, plots our demise, and blindsides us via thoughtless neighbors, inconsiderate drivers, careless clerks, dense husbands, children taking *for–ev–er*. But waiting is an unavoidable part of life, and the Bible says we don't have to be undone by it. The Lord's patience is our shield and defense, and He's got plenty stockpiled.

PRAYER

Sometimes I think I'm like that little girl from *Willy Wonka and the Chocolate Factory*, Lord—the one who cried out, "I want it and I want it now!" When I get my mind set on something, I definitely want it, and the sooner the better. Sometimes—truth be told—I get angry when I have to wait on something that "should be" mine. Then I'm reminded that You're the one in charge of the timing. You're also the one who knows what's best for me, so it's possible You're saying no to my request because it doesn't line up with Your will. Teach me to wait on You and to trust Your judgment. Amen.

Day 345

IN HIS POWER

I can do all things through Christ who strengthens me.
PHILIPPIANS 4:13 NKJV

Need strength? Turn to God for all you need. Why take on life by yourself when He offers you His own power? Often as obedient Christians, we make great efforts with our feeble spiritual muscles. But ultimately our own strength always fails. When Christ's Spirit works through us, the Christian life flows smoothly; in His power, we accomplish His purposes. Today, is Christ bearing the burden, or are we? Only He has the power we need in our lives.

PRAYER

I want people to think I'm trusting You, Lord. But sometimes, if I'm being perfectly honest, I'm really trying to snatch things out of Your hands. I want to take back control because I have momentary lapses in trust. My faith flies out the window when things don't happen as I think they should. But my best efforts can't even come close to Yours, Father! Your power, Your Spirit, Your purposes? They all come together seamlessly when I leave the "doing" up to You. Thank You for that reminder today! Amen.

Day 346

SPROUTS

"For there is hope for a tree, when it is cut down, that it will sprout again."

JOB 14:7 NASB

Have you ever battled a stubborn tree? You know, one you can saw off at the ground but the tenacious thing keeps sprouting new growth from the roots? You have to admire the resiliency of that life force, tenacious in its refusal to give up. That's hope in a nutshell, sisters. We must believe, even as stumps, that eventually we will become majestic, towering evergreens if we just keep sending out those sprouts.

PRAYER

There have been times when I was cut off from the roots up, Lord. When I thought I would never sprout again. I felt like my days of usefulness were over. Hopelessness creeped in. But then, when I least expected it, a little sprout shot up out of the ground. I found myself marveling at the new growth, even questioning it. Was it truly possible, after all this time, that a new season was beginning for me? Now I see that You are the God of the seasons. I trust You to bring new things to life, Lord, and to keep using me for Your glory! Amen.

Day 347

YOU WILL PROSPER

Do not turn from [the Book of the Law]. . . , that you may prosper. . . . You shall meditate in it day and night.
JOSHUA 1:7–8 NKJV

God promised success to Joshua if he obeyed His Word. That promise applies to you too. But sometimes you may not feel that obeying God has brought you great prosperity. Just wait. It may take time, the success may not take the form you expect, or you may not see the results until you reach heaven, but God will prosper those who do His will. He promised it, and His promises never fail.

PRAYER

I often find myself waiting on the "prospering" part, Lord. But I'm learning that You require obedience during those waiting seasons. If Joshua hadn't continued to march around Jericho, those walls never would have fallen. But he kept going, day after day, and in the end he won the battle. I'll win if I don't give up. And I don't plan on waving the white flag. I want to keep marching, keep hoping, keep believing. Because I know—at some point when I least suspect it—You're going to instruct me to give the victory shout! Amen.

Day 348

GETTING TO KNOW YOU

For the law never made anything perfect.
But now we have confidence in a better hope,
through which we draw near to God.
HEBREWS 7:19 NLT

Following Old Testament law used to be considered the way to achieve righteousness, but obeying rules just doesn't work for fallible humans. We mess up. We fail miserably. Then Jesus came and provided a better way to draw near to God. He bridged the gap by offering us a personal relationship rather than rules. Together we laugh, cry, love, grieve, rejoice. We get to know our Papa God through our personal relationship with Him.

PRAYER

I've tried following the rules, Lord. Despite my best attempts, I still fall short. I miss the mark. And then I beat myself up because I see myself as a failure. That's no way to live. Thank You for breaking us free from the cycle of guilt and blame. I'm grateful for my relationship with You, which provides a better way to live. You long for relationship. So do I! You're not judging all of the things I get wrong. On the contrary, You're loving me so beautifully that I want to respond with a life well lived. What a wonderful way to enjoy life! Amen.

Day 349

REAL SUCCESS

O Lord, save now, we beseech You; O Lord, we beseech You, send now prosperity and give us success!

Psalm 118:25 AMP

Is it wrong to pray for success? No. But notice that the Bible connects success to God's salvation. Prosperity or any other achievement means little when it's separated from God's will and our obedience to Him. When you ask to attain something, do you also seek God's saving grace in that part of your life? If so, you'll have real success—spiritual and temporal blessings.

PRAYER

Temporary blessings are nice, Lord, but they flit in and out in no time at all. Sure, I'm happy in the moment, but ultimately I long for true success—not the kind the world has to offer, but the fruit of a life well lived. When I submit my whole heart to You, submitting every part of my life to Your will and Your way, the blessings aren't temporary. They're eternal. I get to walk from this life straight into eternity with You. To my way of thinking, the most "prosperous" life is the one fully surrendered to You. Amen.

Day 350

NOTHING MORE THAN FEELINGS

Lord, sustain me as you promised, that I may live! Do not let my hope be crushed.

Psalm 119:116 NLT

Whatever our foe—unemployment, rejection, loss, illness—we may feel beaten down by life. Our hope feels crushed by the relentless boulder bearing down on our souls. We feel that we can't possibly endure another day. Yes, we feel. But feelings are often deceiving. God promises to sustain us, to strengthen us so that we might withstand that massive rock. We can trust Him. He will not allow us to be crushed!

PRAYER

Feelings have proven to be deceptive time and time again. But I've fallen for them, Lord. I've given in to them and let them rule my actions and my responses. Thank You for the reminder that I am not to be controlled by my feelings. They can't carry the full weight of the battle. What's more, they will steer me in the wrong direction. Instead, I will lean on Your promises. They never fail me. They are there to sustain and keep me no matter what I'm facing. How grateful I am to have something stronger than my feelings to hold on to! Amen.

Day 351

LEAN ON JESUS

"Therefore if the Son makes you free, you shall be free indeed."
JOHN 8:36 NKJV

Sometimes we don't feel freed from sin. Temptations entice us, even though we love Jesus. So His words here can be both comforting and challenging. The Jews wanted to trust in their spiritual history, not in God. That plan didn't work well for them, and it won't work for us either. We can't rely on history or our past deeds to put sin behind us. What will work? Leaning on Jesus every day, trusting Him to make us free indeed!

PRAYER

"Set free." How I love those words, Jesus! You set me free when You took my sin and shame to the cross with You. Unfortunately, I sometimes pick those things back up again. I slip them on like a winter jacket and wear them, in spite of my relationship with You. I get stuck on the wrong things I did in the past. I can't seem to let them go, in spite of Your forgiveness. Thank You for the reminder that I don't have to go on feeling stuck. You set me free. . .and I'm free indeed. I don't have to succumb to temptation. I can rise above it and move on! Amen.

Day 352

REDEEMED!

Israel, wait for the LORD; for with the LORD there is mercy, and with Him is abundant redemption.

PSALM 130:7 NASB

The psalmist knew Israel had a rotten track record. Throughout Old Testament history, God miraculously delivered the Israelites from trouble repeatedly and they would turn gratefully to Him, only to eventually slip again into rebellion and more trouble. Sounds a lot like you and me, doesn't it? But thankfully, ours is a redemptive God. A God who offers abundant loving-kindness and forgiveness. A God of second chances—then and now.

PRAYER

Thank You for being such a redemptive God! How many times have I broken Your heart only to have You fold me into Your arms again, offering forgiveness and grace? You always respond with loving-kindness, no matter how badly I've fallen off course. What a deep, deep love You have for us, Lord, one I simply can't comprehend. I want to. I want to offer friends and family the same kind of grace-filled love, but it's not easy. So I'll learn from You, lean on You, and do my best to emulate You, heavenly Father. Amen.

Day 353

APPRECIATION OVERFLOW

Continue to live your lives in [Jesus], rooted and built up in him, strengthened in the faith as you were taught, and overflowing with thankfulness.

COLOSSIANS 2:6–7 NIV

Strong Christians are thankful Christians. As we realize all Jesus has sacrificed for us and appreciate our inability to live the Christian life on our own, we remember to praise our Savior for His grace. Today we can be rooted in Jesus, strong in our faith, and thankful to the one who has given us these blessings. Let's overflow with appreciation!

PRAYER

I have so much to be grateful for, Lord. You've blessed me abundantly—with my life, my health, my family, and so many other things. And though I don't always remember to thank You, I'm forever grateful for every single thing. Show me how to live an appreciative life, one filled with gratitude to You and to others. May I radiate appreciation to all I come in contact with. And may I learn from Your example, knowing that the greatest blessing of all is the love I show others along the way. Amen.

Day 354

MR. CLEAN FOR THE SOUL

As far as the east is from the west, so far has He removed our wrongdoings from us.

PSALM 103:12 NASB

Dirty little secrets. We all have them. Exposing them is a popular theme for television shows these days. But we don't have to wallow in the muck of our past. God has promised to wash us clean of our dirty little secrets and remove them as far as the east is from the west when we repent of our wrongdoings and ask Him for forgiveness. An immaculate and sparkling fresh start—repentance is Mr. Clean for the soul!

PRAYER

I get so ashamed when I think about my dirty little secrets, Lord. The things I've done in the dark that no one knows about. The icky things I've said and thought about others. So many indiscretions. I could get stuck there, in the mire of yesterday, but You encourage me not to. You say I should step into today, washed clean of the sins of the past. You say that repentance changes everything, so today I choose to come clean, to start anew, to walk into an amazing future filled with fresh starts. Thanks for cleansing me, Lord! Amen.

Day 355

FOREVER THANKFUL

Oh, give thanks to the LORD, for He is good!
For His mercy endures forever.
PSALM 136:1 NKJV

Now, honestly, how do you respond to this call for thanks? Does your heart leap at the opportunity, or does it just hit you with a dull thud? Why is it so important to thank God? Because He will always be merciful to you. Whether you rejoice easily or you find yourself having to work up some enthusiasm, if you have trusted in the Savior, He still loves you. Isn't that something wonderful to give thanks for?

PRAYER

More often than not, I need to be reminded before I muster up gratitude for the blessings You send my way, Lord. I'm ashamed that I live such a thankless life. I rarely spontaneously offer thanksgiving for all You've done for me. But You say I don't have to be ashamed. I can start right here, right now. So here goes! I praise You, Lord! You've been so good to me, and You are deserving of all my praise! May it rise like a song from my heart, an offering of thanksgiving to a God who has poured Himself out on my behalf. How grateful I am to You, my Savior! Amen.

Day 356

COUNTING ON IT

Blessed is the one who perseveres under trial because, having stood the test, that person will receive the crown of life that the Lord has promised to those who love him.

JAMES 1:12 NIV

Some think that when you turn your life over to Christ, all your troubles are over. But if you've been a believer for more than a day, you'll realize that the Christian life is no Caribbean cruise. There will be trials; there will be tribulations. Count on it. But Jesus promises a glorious reward for our perseverance through those hard times. Count on that even more.

PRAYER

Sometimes I feel like "perseverance" is my theme song, Lord. It's the undercurrent of so many of my days. My life has been tough. Some seasons were a lot rougher than expected. I've found myself distressed during times of tribulation. But You've never let me linger there for long. In Your gentle, loving way You always reach down and whisper, "Keep going, kid!" And I do. I put one foot in front of the other and move forward, hard as it may seem. Thank You for teaching me that perseverance is growing me into a woman of strength! Amen.

Day 357

GOD CALLS US TO JOY

Consider it pure joy, my brothers and sisters, whenever you face trials of many kinds.

JAMES 1:2 NIV

Joy? To be faced with trials should cause us joy? Hard to imagine, isn't it? But God calls us to joy when unbelievers persecute us because of our faith or when our situation is merely difficult. He is overjoyed when we stand firm in our faith, and He calls us to share His delight. That doesn't mean we seek out trials but rather that we face each hard situation hand in hand with God. In trials our spiritual strength increases.

PRAYER

I will count it all joy, Lord. Even when my circumstances don't make sense. Even when tears are streaming down my face. I'll consider it joy because I know—in the end—You will use this situation for my good and Your glory. You will grow me into a woman who is much stronger than before. And You will give me life lessons I couldn't have learned any other way. Trials will come and go, but the joy that comes from knowing You? It's going to last all of my days and throughout eternity. Thank You for making me a woman of joy, Father! Amen.

Day 358

OVERFLOWING LOVE

Precious in the sight of the Lord *is the death of His godly ones.*

Psalm 116:15 NASB

"Jesus wept." Two small words that portray the enormity of Jesus' emotion following the death of His dear friend Lazarus (John 11:35). Jesus knew Lazarus wouldn't stay dead, that he'd soon miraculously rise from the grave. So why did Jesus weep? The depth of His love for those precious to Him overflowed. Our Lord grieves with us in our losses today and comforts us with the knowledge that His beloved will rise to eternal life in heaven.

PRAYER

Oh, how I've grieved for my loved ones who've crossed over into heaven, Lord. Not for their current situation, of course. They're now enjoying the bliss of Your presence. But I've grieved for myself, knowing it may be years before I see them again. I wonder sometimes how nonbelievers survive the death of a loved one. I couldn't bear the idea of never seeing loved ones again. I'm so grateful for the promise of heaven and the joy of knowing that one day I will see my dear ones again. Thank You for that promise for all believers. Amen.

Day 359

HE CARES!

The righteous cry out, and the LORD hears,
and delivers them out of all their troubles.
PSALM 34:17 NKJV

As God's child, you have His ear 24-7 if only you will pray. Every need, trouble, or praise is His concern. And not only will He hear about your trials, He will deliver you from them. Feel discouraged by the hardships you're facing? You need not stay that way. Just spend time with Jesus. His help is on the way.

PRAYER

I've often wondered if people really hear what I say to them, Lord. Are they even paying attention? They respond with a "Sure" or a "Yeah," but their eyes have a faraway look. You, though? You're always on the job, listening to every word. And best of all, You truly care about what I'm saying. It matters to You because I matter to You. And You're already working on a plan to help me through the very things I'm talking to You about. I'm so grateful for the caring way You love me, Lord! Thank You. Amen.

Day 360

GUILT-FREE

"I will forgive their wickedness, and I will never again remember their sins."

HEBREWS 8:12 NLT

Guilt. It tends to consume us women to the point that many of the things we do are motivated by guilt. But God says we don't have to allow guilt to control us. We should learn from past mistakes, certainly, and then shed the guilt like a moth-eaten winter coat. Don a fresh spring outfit and look ahead. Our past prepares us for the future if we are open to the present.

PRAYER

There was a time when guilt was the steering wheel in my proverbial car, Lord. It literally drove me everywhere. I couldn't seem to escape it. People would say, "She carries the guilt of the world on her shoulders." And that was definitely true. I'm not sure why I always felt so guilty. . .about everything. Maybe it was my works-based upbringing? Regardless, I'm so glad to finally be rid of that pesky guilt! It torments me no longer. I've been set free, once and for all, now that I fully understand Your forgiveness and grace. I praise You for freedom, Lord. Amen.

Day 361

GOD'S COMPASSIONATE SALVATION

Do not repay anyone evil for evil. Be careful to do what is right in the eyes of everyone.
ROMANS 12:17 NIV

Tit-for-tat retribution for evil is not a principle of our compassionate God. We understand this if we've received His undeserved salvation. With such a gift, God has opened our hearts to treating our enemies as He has treated us. If we refuse to count up each wrong and repay it with harshness, lost souls may understand God's compassionate salvation. By doing right, even when we receive wrong in return, we become powerful witnesses.

PRAYER

The word *Justice* has become a viral term, hasn't it, Lord? Everyone wants justice. And I get it. Life is unfair. But it seems to me that a lot of people are seeking justice for things they should simply talk through with a friend. Little things that don't require a tit-for-tat response. Things that could be settled with a conversation over a cup of coffee. Help me to always be willing to do the right thing, even when those around me aren't. I'm more interested in pleasing Your heart than in proving some kind of point or winning an argument. Please help me. Amen.

Day 362

CLOSE TO YOU

I stay close to you, and your powerful arm supports me.
PSALM 63:8 CEV

There's an old saying: "I used to be close to God, but someone moved." If God is the same yesterday, today, and tomorrow, He's not the one going anywhere. So how do we stay close to God? So close that His powerful arm supports us, protects us, and lifts us up when we're down? The answer is prayer—as a lifestyle, as something as much a part of ourselves as breathing. Prayer isn't just spiritual punctuation; it's every word of our life story.

PRAYER

I confess, there have been many times when I said the words, "God feels so far away." I felt that deeply during the darker moments, when I walked through grief or pain. I can see now that You hadn't moved. You were right there, wanting to hold me, comfort me, bring healing. But I was so closed off that I couldn't see You, Lord. Thank You for the reminder that You're not going anywhere, even when I'm in the deepest pit. When I need You most, You're right there, arms extended, ready to lift me up to begin again. Thank You, Lord! Amen.

Day 363

A RIGHT RELATIONSHIP WITH GOD

May the righteous be glad and rejoice before God; may they be happy and joyful.
PSALM 68:3 NIV

Many women believe that happiness is a result of success. "When I find the right person to marry, I'll be happy." "When I achieve my career goals. . ." "When I can afford the home I really want. . ." The truth is that real happiness—deep inner joy—is the result of living in right relationship with God rather than having the trappings of success. Regardless of what you may be facing—good and bad—be happy knowing you are pleasing your heavenly Father.

PRAYER

Heavenly Father, I'll admit that I've wasted a lot of time chasing after that "next big thing" that's sure to bring happiness and lasting contentment into my life. I've learned the hard way that no matter what I achieve, I still want more—something bigger and better—and so I keep on striving for what's next. The endless chase is exhausting and frustrating. Help me to slow down and focus on chasing what really matters: a right relationship with You, Lord. When I get that right, everything else will fall into place. My soul will truly know joy and contentment that nothing else in the world can replicate. Amen.

Day 364

RAISING OUR HOPES

"Did I ask you for a son, my lord?" she said.
"Didn't I tell you, 'Don't raise my hopes'?"
2 KINGS 4:28 NIV

Are you afraid to raise your hope in God's provision for fear that hope will crash and burn? The woman from Shunem had everything but her heart's desire—a child. She was afraid to believe Elisha's prediction of her pregnancy, but his prayerful intervention made her dream come true. When the boy later died, however, she lashed out. God restored her son and raised her hope from the dead. Literally. Dare we raise our hopes too?

PRAYER

It seems scary sometimes, Lord, to get my hopes up. Maybe that's because I've had them dashed so many, many times. Mostly by people, of course; but there were times when I blamed You, albeit falsely. I wondered why things didn't work out, and I grew bitter. Thank You for the reminder that You can lift my eyes and my heart. You can give me reason to hope again, even when things don't appear promising in the natural. Most of all, I praise You for being a God of hope, one who sees my needs through eyes of love. Amen.

Day 365

THE SOURCE OF SALVATION

He became the source of eternal salvation for all who obey him.
HEBREWS 5:9 NIV

Salvation in Jesus is important to our earthly lives. How many times has He dispelled danger or helped us avoid it? How often has sin been kept from marring our lives because we obeyed His commands? But Jesus is also the source of salvation in eternity. Instead of having us remain forever in our earthly lives, God planned to bring us into everlasting life with Him in His restored kingdom. In heaven, we will praise His salvation without end!

PRAYER

Eternity started for me the day I asked You to come live in my heart, Jesus! Every moment from then until now has been part of my eternal journey. Heaven is going to be beyond amazing, of course, but I don't want to wait until then to celebrate. I'll start right here, right now. Why? Because I know You love me and have great plans for me. You say that I'm loved, I'm valuable to the kingdom, and I'm Your dear child. I was born for great things, and there's no point in waiting another day to experience them. Thank You for eternity, Lord! Amen.

SCRIPTURE INDEX

OLD TESTAMENT

NEW TESTAMENT

Acts

Romans

1 Corinthians

2 Corinthians